CREATION
AT THE
CROSSROADS

A Small-Group Resource
on Pope Francis'
Laudato Si'

(On Care for Our Common Home)

EDWARD J. CIUBA

RENEW
INTERNATIONAL

Quotations from *Laudato Si'* (*On Care for Our Common Home*) © 2015 Libreria Editrice Vaticana.

For resources related to *Creation at the Crossroads,* visit www.renewintl.org/renewearth

NIHIL OBSTAT
Censor Librorum
Rev. Msgr. C. Anthony Ziccardi, S.S.L., S.T.D.

IMPRIMATUR
Most Reverend John J. Myers, J.C.D., D.D.
Archbishop of Newark

Cover design by Ruth Markworth

Text design by Kathrine Kuo

ISBN: 978-1-62063-113-3

RENEW International
1232 George Street
Plainfield, NJ 07062-1717
www.renewintl.org

Printed and bound in the United States of America

Printed on 100% recycled paper

Contents

Presenting RENEW International

The RENEW process, both parish-based and diocese-wide, was first developed and implemented in the Archdiocese of Newark, New Jersey. Its success there led other dioceses, in the United States and in other countries, to bring RENEW to their people and parish communities.

In the three decades since its vibrant beginnings, RENEW International has touched the lives of 25 million people in over 150 dioceses in the United States and 24 countries throughout the world.

RENEW International has grown organically from its original single RENEW process. Materials and training have been inculturated and made available in over 40 languages. We have added specific pastoral outreach to campuses and to young adults in their 20s and 30s. We have incorporated prison ministry and provided resources for the visually impaired.

The very core of all of these processes remains the same: to help people become better hearers and doers of the Word of God. We do this by encouraging and supporting the formation of small communities who gather prayerfully to reflect on and share the Word of God, to make better connections between faith and life, and to live their faith more concretely in family, work, and community life.

As a not-for-profit organization, we sustain our pastoral outreach in part from the sales of our publications and resources and the stipends we receive for the services provided to parishes and dioceses. However, our priority is always to serve all parishes who desire to renew their faith and build the Church, regardless of their economic situation. We have been able to fulfill this mission not only in the inner city and rural areas in the United States but also in the developing world, especially Latin America and Africa, thanks to donations and charitable funding.

As you meet in your small group, we invite you to take a few moments to imagine the great invisible network of others here in the United States and on the other continents. They gather, as you do, in small Christian communities, around the Word of God present in the Scripture, striving to hear and act upon that Word. Keep them in your prayer: a prayer of thanksgiving for the many graces we have experienced; a prayer that the Spirit will guide all of us through *Creation at the Crossroads.*

Foreword

I was privileged to be asked to speak at the Vatican launch of *Laudato Si'*, Pope Francis' encyclical on caring for God's creation. Many refer to that as his "climate change encyclical," but that shorthand does a disservice to the document by framing it as focused on only one environmental concern.

Certainly the encyclical deals with the very important issue of global warming and the scientific consensus around that, but it does so much more, calling on all of us to look at creation "as a gift from the outstretched hand of the Father of all, and as a reality illuminated by the love which calls us together into universal communion." It asks us to change our attitude towards that gift, realize that we all share it, we all need it, we are all in this world together.

Look at how the Holy Father opens his document, explaining that its title—which translates "Praise Be!" —comes from the canticle written by the saint whose name the pope adopted:

"In the words of this beautiful canticle, Saint Francis of Assisi reminds us that our common home is like a sister with whom we share our life and a beautiful mother who opens her arms to embrace us ... This sister now cries out to us because of the harm we have inflicted on her by our irresponsible use and abuse of the goods with which God has endowed her" (*Laudato Si'*, 1).

For us at Catholic Relief Services, the parts of *Laudato Si'* that ring so true are those that make clear the impact that imprudent decisions and actions have on the poor. These issues, including climate change, are not abstract arguments for us. They are a daily reality for the people we work with around the world, people who have not created these problems but are suffering the most from them.

We see rising waters threaten homes in Bangladesh. We see more powerful storms devastate communities in the Philippines. We see changing rainfall patterns lead to food shortages in West Africa. We see rising temperatures cause traditional crops to fail in Central America.

These are not people who can move to higher ground. They cannot go to the grocery store and buy more food if none comes from their garden plot. They cannot shut the door and turn up the air conditioner if the temperature rises. These are life-and-death issues for them.

But Pope Francis does not despair. His encyclical gives us hope that all of us can change this course if we come to an understanding of our role in God's creation. The pope reassures us that our bountiful and generous God has given us a world that can sustain us all in health and dignity. If we find, as we are today, that it is not sustaining us, the blame is on our own shoulders. For example, the Holy Father tells us, "To blame population growth instead of extreme and selective consumerism on the part of some, is one way of refusing to face the issues. It is an attempt to legitimize the present model of distribution, where a minority believes that it has the right to consume in a way which can never be universalized, since the planet could not even contain the waste products of such consumption" (50).

Pope Francis writes about our "throwaway culture." One example of this is something we have all seen—decisions made for short-term gains that are detrimental in the long run. This sort of selfish behavior must end. We all must examine our lives, our decisions, to see their implications for our shared world. Think always of this: What kind of world do you want to leave your children?

Sometimes climate-caused problems do land on our doorsteps, but we do not realize that their origin is in the mistreatment of our world. Many of the refugees in Europe would still be at home if they could grow crops to feed their families. Many of the displaced on our borders are fleeing violent, gang-ridden cities in Central America crowded with those who have left farms that are no longer fertile.

I congratulate RENEW International, the Catholic Climate Covenant, and GreenFaith for bringing the encyclical to life in parishes, religious communities, and college campuses by publishing this resource, *Creation at the Crossroads*.

As you use this book to reflect on *Laudato Si'*, please consider, first, what can be done to take better care of God's creation and, second, how we can help those suffering most from the consequences of climate change to live with dignity in their changed environment. Both are important.

By opening this book you are taking an important first step, beginning what Pope Francis in *Laudato Si'* calls "a new dialogue about how we are shaping the future of our planet." The pope goes on to say, "We need a conversation which includes everyone, since the environmental challenge we are undergoing, and its human roots, concern and affect us all" (14).

Let such conversations be the first steps of many that you take on this journey to a world whose bounty is shared with justice and mercy.

Dr. Carolyn Y. Woo
President and CEO
Catholic Relief Services

Introduction

Immediately after Cardinal Jorge Bergoglio was elected pope on March 13, 2013, he was asked, "What name do you take?"

"Francis," he responded.

Some thought they misheard. "Did he say Francis?" No other pope had taken that name! How curious that a Jesuit would have chosen the name of the founder of the Franciscans, St. Francis of Assisi. On the other hand, given the importance of the virtue of discernment in Jesuit spirituality, Cardinal Bergoglio could hardly have chosen the name of Francis without prior reflection and prayer.

Whatever the illuminating source, the new pontiff, Francis, was sending a message, a plan, and a vision for the future. The name "Francis" was well chosen. Even as archbishop of Buenos Aires, he was acquainted with the slums of that capital city, as he was with its public subway system that took him to work daily. He eschewed a private car, which would have been acceptable, given his age and position. He lived frugally. He admired the example of his sainted namesake, St. Francis, "Il Poverello," who left behind a life of luxury, cared for the poor, preached simplicity of life, and reverenced the sacredness and beauty of Mother Earth.

Like St. Francis, whom Jesus called in a dream to "rebuild my Church" in the thirteenth century, was Pope Francis intimating that he was being called to do the same for the Church of the twenty-first century? In the early days of his pontificate, he indicated his desire to reform and to modernize the Church. He began with the Vatican bank. Then he followed by establishing structures to allow for currents of change, reshaping the Roman Curia. Above all, Pope Francis' concern was to proclaim anew the Good News of Jesus Christ with the vigor, courage, simplicity, and joy of a new pastoral vision for the entire Body of Christ. Such was the intent of his apostolic exhortation, *Evangelii Gaudium* (*The Joy of the Gospel*).

In one of his first talks to media representatives, in Rome on March 16, 2013, Pope Francis said, "I chose the name of Francis because for me St. Francis is a man of poverty, a man of peace, a man who loves and protects creation. These days we do not have a very good relationship with creation, do we?"

In a similar vein, at his inaugural papal Mass on the feast of St. Joseph, March 19, he reflected in his homily: "To protect Jesus with Mary, to protect the whole of creation, to protect each person, especially the poorest, to

Pope St. John Paul II visited 129 countries during the 37 years of his pontificate. Undoubtedly, such extensive international exposure made him sensitive to the major ecological problems that the world was facing. His encyclical, *On Social Concerns,* issued in 1987, was the first substantive papal discussion of ecology; in that document he connected ecology with human dignity, and respect for the earth with personal morality. In his New Year message in 1990 he wrote, "Christians, in particular, realize that their responsibility within creation and their duty towards God and Creator are an essential part of their faith." In other words, concern for creation is not an option; it is a core aspect of faith.

In 2004, at the request of John Paul II, the Pontifical Council for Justice and Peace published the *Compendium of the Social Doctrine of the Church.* The tenth chapter is entitled "Safeguarding the Environment," and it liberally draws on the pope's work. It includes this admonition: "Care for the environment represents a challenge for all of humanity. It is a matter of a common and universal duty, that of respecting a common good."

These are some of Pope St. John Paul's insights:

- We are not "masters" of our planet, only its "faithful and prudent caretakers."

- We must take into account the nature of all created realities and their mutual connection within an ordered system. Such a principle is founded on belief in a Creator God who made all things and judged them to be "good."

- The natural resources of the earth are limited. They are to be cared for, safeguarded, not abused, wasted, or treated as mere for-profit commodities or for personal self-aggrandizement.

- A lack of appreciation for the goodness of creation and the dignity of all people lies at the root of the ecological crisis facing the world. The environmental challenges we face represent a spiritual and moral test.

- "Ecological conversion," i.e., a change of minds, hearts, and attitudes, is necessary if we are to reverse the trend of environmental deterioration and failure to live sustainably on the earth.

protect ourselves: This is a service that the Bishop of Rome is called to carry out, yet one to which all of us are called, so that the star of hope will shine brightly. Let us protect with love all that God has given us."

Does the publication of Pope Francis' major encyclical on the environment indicate a new shift in direction? Or, is he building upon, expanding, and giving a new impetus to long-held truths of Scripture and Tradition as well as the spoken and written words of his predecessors, Pope St. John Paul II and Pope Benedict XVI?

The answer to both parts of the question is yes. Yes, Pope Francis does reveal a "shift," insofar as his first major encyclical focuses entirely on a critical ecological issue that confronts today's world: The role of faith in countering global inequality and the destruction of the environment.

However, this is not a new "shift." His encyclical, continues, builds upon and expands the initiatives of the previous two popes. But Francis' personal charisma combined with the urgency of the crisis posed by climate change has given the topic of caring for the earth a renewed vitality. The pope's commitment has been felt in the following ways:

— By consciously adopting the name "Francis," with all that it symbolizes, he gives the full moral weight and authority of the papacy to a renewed vision for healing the earth and giving hope to inhabitants of this imperiled planet.

— This encyclical is the first document addressed by a pope to the entire Catholic community and to all other people of good conscience exclusively on topics of ecology and the environment.

— The pope's initiative also marks a highly visible coming together of religion and science to convey the message that protecting the environment is, in the words of UN Secretary-General Ban Ki-moon, "a sacred duty for all people of faith and people of conscience."

— The encyclical expresses an urgent concern about the deteriorating condition of our planet and the impact on poor and otherwise marginalized people. Difficult decisions confront developing countries regarding fundamental life issues such as water, clean air, and availability of food. *Laudato Si'* inspires a much-needed synergy among government and political leaders, churches, and scientific and ecological organizations representing the entire world.

— Pope Francis has made the relationship between care for creation, integral human development, and concern for poor people a core issue of his pontificate. He and many of those who served as consultants and contributors to the encyclical represent developing nations in Africa, Asia, and Central and South America. Their voices add a quality of personal, lived experience that resonates with the daily lives of millions of people in less developed countries.

Early in his pontificate, Benedict XVI was dubbed the "Green Pope" by a number of Vatican observers. Throughout his time in office, he sounded this theme: Awaken your consciences. Look at how our earth is being impoverished and abused. As a believer, you have the responsibility to do something—to act.

In fact, in his inaugural homily he urged pastors and religious leaders to make their congregations aware of how their environment was being ravaged: "The earth's treasures no longer serve to build God's garden for all to live in," he said, "but they have been made to serve the powers of exploitation and destruction."

During his tenure, the Vatican City State became the world's first "carbon-neutral" country, meaning that greenhouse-gas omissions are offset by renewable energy and carbon credits through reforestation projects. Also, the Paul VI auditorium in Vatican City, which accommodates 6,000 people, was equipped with 2,400 solar panels that convert sunlight into some 300,000 kilowatt-hours of energy each year

At Benedict's request, in August 2006, all of the parishes in Italy celebrated a first-ever "Call for Commitment to Creation Day." His words were clear: "Creation is exposed to serious risks by lifestyles and choices that can degrade it. Environmental degradation makes the lives of the poor especially vulnerable."

Pope Benedict indicated often his concern that the Church had forgotten about "creation theology." By this he meant that the theology of creation and redemption must be seen together. The same God who creates also redeems the world. The full meaning of creation and the importance of the environment and all living and non-living species could not be fully understood without God's coming into an earthly context in the person of Jesus Christ. People who are conscious of a redeeming Creator must strive to save creation and not destroy it.

"Environmental justice," the application of Catholic social principles to issues of care for the earth, is a relatively new term. The topic was first addressed in some of the social encyclicals of St. John Paul II whose pontificate began in 1978—only thirty-seven years ago. As far back as the beginning of the Industrial Revolution in the late nineteenth century, the Church, through its popes, has addressed many of the theological and moral issues of the times such as the protection of human rights for laborers, rejection of movements and organizations that failed to recognize the dignity of the human person, industrialization, capitalism, socialism, Marxism, the relationship between rich and poor nations, and a broad range of other social issues.

But it was only within these past five decades that more and more voices in society were recognizing how the natural world was being abused and its limited resources were becoming unsustainably depleted. It was in the context of such a world that Popes St. John Paul II and Benedict XVI recognized that faith and moral principles are essential to offset the rampant degradation of nature and destruction of life. The Church's prioritization of ecology and care for the earth under Pope Francis had begun to emerge strongly in the teaching of the previous two popes.

The twelve faith-sharing sessions which will follow aim to bring people together to read, reflect, pray, and then to share on the central points and practical applications of the encyclical. Our objective is to help Catholics internalize, and set as a priority in their lives, the Church's teaching on the care of creation and the impact of environmental change on those who are poor and vulnerable. You too can learn more about the ecological challenges of our times and do something about them.

About the Author

Edward J. Ciuba is a priest of the Archdiocese of Newark. He was a professor of biblical studies at Immaculate Conception Seminary and then served as rector of the seminary at Mahwah (Darlington), NJ, and then at Seton Hall University, South Orange, NJ. Father Ciuba is the author of *Who Do You Say That I Am?* and *Why Should We Care About Planet Earth, Our Home?* He is in residence at Church of the Presentation, Upper Saddle River, NJ, where he is member of the St. Francis Eco-spirituality Committee. He is a frequent speaker on Scripture, ecology, and spirituality.

Faith Sharing in a Small Group

Welcome to *Creation at the Crossroads: A Small-Group Resource on Pope Francis' Laudato Si' (On Care for Our Common Home)*. In a vision that embraces the human person and the natural environment in all their dimensions, Pope Francis establishes as a top priority for Catholics, and for all people, care for God's creation and lessening of human activity that harms living things and natural resources. Designed for use in parishes and on college campuses, *Creation at the Crossroads* will bring the encyclical into the lives of thousands of people. It will help members of parishes and faith communities understand the encyclical's teachings and apply them to their lives.

Social Inquiry Approach: See, Judge, Act

In *Laudato Si'*, Pope Francis has employed a method of social inquiry known as "See, Judge Act"—a method used by previous popes in other social encyclicals. Pope St. John XXIII, in his encyclical *Mater et Magistra*, explained the use of these three steps to transform social principles into practical action: "First, one reviews the concrete situation; secondly, one forms a judgment on it in the light of these same principles; thirdly, one decides what in the circumstances can and should be done to implement these principles" (*Mater et Magistra*, 236, May 15, 1961).

— In Chapter 1 of his encyclical, Pope Francis describes the current reality (See).

— In Chapters 2, 3, and 4, he looks at the deeper reality in light of Scripture and certain cultural trends, and he lays out an alternative vision of integral ecology (Judge).

— In Chapters 5 and 6, he identifies two levels of action: the need for leadership and regulation and the need for radical change in lifestyles— an ecological conversion (Act).

The "See, Judge, Act" approach was adopted by Cardinal Joseph Cardijn, who was a Belgian priest when he founded the Young Christian Workers (YCW) after World War I. The YCW sought to enable young workers to re-Christianize their own lives, their working and social environments, and individuals with whom they worked.

The movement took root in the United States as the Young Christian Students (YCS) and the Christian Family Movement (CFM). The latter still works to to promote family life centered on Christ, help people live their Christian faith in everyday life; and improve society through action, education, and example. The CFM encourages the formation of small Christian communities that can transform parishes and the wider society.

RENEW International also uses the "See, Judge, Act" method in *Creation at the Crossroads*. Here is how the method is applied in small-group meetings:

See

The "See" portion of the meeting is designed to help the group face facts. This part of the meeting does not consist of a discussion based on personal opinions; instead, the "See" step helps participants focus their attention on the reality of the situation. Each session of *Creation at the Crossroads* includes a true story—an example of the reality of the situation— that is related to the theme of the session.

Judge

The "Judge" aspect is the crux of the meeting. During this time, participants reflect on and share their responses to a passage from Scripture and a written discussion that treats more deeply, in light of Scripture and the teachings of the Church, the subject illustrated by the opening story. This aspect of the meeting may impel members to initiate research that will help them more clearly understand their faith and its application to life and, in particular, to the conditions described in the session. Participants are prompted to ask themselves why a given condition—such as pollution of air and soil or inequitable availability of clean water—is a moral challenge to people in general and to them in particular, and what it has to do with their Christian faith.

The "Judge" aspect benefits from the collective wisdom of the group as consensus emerges from its sharing. This wisdom reflects the activity of the Holy Spirit, alive in the community members. This process of reflection and judgment takes a practical turn. Theory alone will not enable people to bring about change in a given situation. Down-to-earth considerations such as whom to approach and what to say must be taken into account. The collective wisdom of a group usually avoids ill-advised efforts and results in a practical and effective response to the situation at hand. When the "Judge" part of the process is done well, it usually leads naturally to meaningful action.

The leader may very well introduce questions such as the following in the "Judge" portion of the meeting:

- What can we do about the situation or condition we have discussed?

- How can we go about changing the attitudes and behaviors that have led to this condition?

- In what way will our own actions reflect Scripture and the teaching of the Church?

Act

The sharing at each meeting leads to commitment to specific actions. These may be individual actions or ones taken by the group as a whole. The scope of these actions is not a prime concern. What is important is that the proposed actions are practical, concrete, and possible to accomplish. It is also important that group members choose actions that flow from prayer, sharing, and their life experiences. This part of the session should not conclude until the leader has determined, either explicitly or implicitly, that every member has a specific action in mind.

The action can be as simple as having a conversation in the coming week that will raise a particular topic with the aim of influencing an attitude. The action can also be a very significant action representing the united commitment of the entire small Christian community. Over the period of weeks, sufficient time for research and analysis of the social concern in question and the development of a total commitment of the small community to a long-term action of considerable proportion can take place.

Being as specific as possible aids the process. For example, having a particular person in mind to talk to and having an exact time when the subject will be brought up improves the probability that a participant will follow through. The more specific the action, the greater the chance of actually doing it. Breaking the ice, by courageously performing small actions on a regular basis, usually leads people, in time, to significant involvement and real leadership.

At the beginning of each session, beginning with the second, members of the group share briefly the outcome of the action they committed to at the previous meeting. These brief reports serve to encourage the group members and give them a sense of progress. Each session offers some examples of possible actions, but the experience is best when participants choose actions of their own.

Some Key Ideas

Some of you have already experienced meeting and sharing in small communities. For others, this may be a new experience. You are coming together as a group, but you are not just meeting together as a discussion or study group where you talk about ideas. Rather, you gather in small Christian communities as a sharing group, open to the Spirit of God, seeking to grow in faith and in your relationship with God and one another.

For all of you engaging in this spiritual adventure together, here are some key ideas that help bring about good, healthy faith sharing.

Gathering

The first fundamental is that you have chosen to gather as a small community to share prayer, life, and faith in a way that will enrich your own lives, the life of your parish community, and the life of the diocese as a community. The members of the small group need to take the time to get to know one another.

Always allow time for introductions at the first session. At later sessions, take a moment or two to ask each other how you are and what has happened since you last met. If anyone new joins the group, again allow time for introductions. Time spent on introductions and checking in is never wasted: the goal is to form a community.

Hospitality and Environment

A welcoming atmosphere is very important for faith sharing. The members of the group need to feel comfortable, physically and psychologically. Effective sharing needs sufficient quiet time with as few distractions as possible. It is good to establish a central focus, using something that will help direct thoughts toward the theme of the session. A small table that displays a candle and other symbolic items contribute to a prayerful atmosphere. For any session it would be extremely appropriate to have a Bible open at the key passage for the session: this emphasizes the central role that the Word of God has in guiding and sharing.

Timing

It is very important to be attentive to the length and pace of each session. Under usual circumstances, a session should last 90 minutes. Most groups then extend their time together in a brief social. The time together in the session should have a balance of prayer, talking about our own experience, exploring Scripture, reflection, faith sharing, and talking about ways of living out our faith. This balance is presented in more detail on pages xxi-xxii.

Prayer

Prayer can and should take different forms. Invite different members of the group to lead prayer. Do not forget that silence is a very important part of any prayer, so build moments of quiet into the time of prayer, with a gentle but explicit prompt from whoever is leading the prayer. For example:

Let us spend a few moments in quiet,
becoming more aware of God's presence ...
... God's presence in each one of us,
and especially in this community,
gathered in Jesus' name.

Songs are suggested for the opening prayer, and the songs listed in this book can be found on the *Creation at the Crossroads* digital playlist, created by OCP and available at www.renewintl.org/creation. However, these are only suggestions.

If you can think of a song that is more representative of your small community, then you should substitute that for what we propose.

More detailed guidance for leading prayer can be found in *Leading Prayer in Small Groups* (for details, visit www.renewintl.org).

Experience

Our spiritual lives do not exist without us! Our experience, then, is essential to our spiritual lives. We need to reflect on our story—what we have experienced in our families, in our other relationships—and explore how that relates to the theme of the session.

Each of the 12 sessions begins with a story that is related to the theme of the session and the themes of Pope Francis' encyclical, *Laudato Si' (On Care for Our Common Home)*.

Scripture

Our Jewish and Christian ancestors read their experiences through the eyes of faith, and in them saw the great story of God's loving relationship with his people. This is set out in what we call the Scriptures, the story God reveals to us, most of all through Christ his Son, the eternal Word. The faith-sharing session gives prominence to the Word of God by prompting us to explore Scripture, noticing what word, phrase, or image from it speaks to us. In a word, we share how it has touched our hearts.

We are offered input to help us understand what God is saying to us today. Then we reflect together on our experience, our story and God's story—and above all how the two link together. All are invited to reflect: each person who wishes to share his or her reflection aloud is given the opportunity to do so. No one dominates, and no one need talk unless he or she wants to.

Challenge and Commitment

One of the key components of faith sharing is how we take what we hear and share and live it out in our lives. That is why a moment of challenge is built into every session. We are given the opportunity to respond not just verbally but by making a commitment to a clear and specific action that we see as a consequence of living out the faith expressed in the sharing. At the following meeting, we are invited to share the results of our efforts in living out that commitment.

We live in a hectic, busy world. Making time for outreach or action will not always be easy. The importance of this time of checking in about our commitments provides the opportunity to reassess our priorities. The key question is not so much "Did I do what I said I would?" but rather "Through this activity, did I manage to live out my faith?" This should also make us look to the bigger question of living out our faith in the totality of our lives: in our family, in our other relationships, in our work environment. We may discover that instead of doing "more" it might be more important for us to do "less"! This is the time to look at how we are living the values of Jesus and the Gospel and to identify what needs to change in our behaviors and attitudes.

The Role of the Leader

Each small community will have its leader. In a faith-sharing context, the leader is not someone with all the answers who is there to preach or teach. The leader is a participant, with the particular responsibility of helping the group by

— doing whatever is necessary to prepare for each session. This requires reading over the session in advance so as to be totally at home with the focus, reflection, and questions. Preparing could also include delegating people to prepare the readings that will be used in the session; delegating the person who will lead the prayer; arranging and/or delegating others to plan and arrange the environment

— guiding the group through the faith-sharing process. Gently keeping the sharing focused on the theme of the session. Moving the sharing from one moment to another, so that the balance and overall timing is respected

— listening, and being prepared to ask questions that will keep the faith sharing moving yet focused

— ensuring that every participant who wants to speak has the opportunity to do so

— being attentive to the dynamics of the group interaction, and providing useful guidance if the group becomes distracted.

More detailed suggestions for the leader are included in *Sowing Seeds: Essentials for Small Community Leaders* (for more details, visit www.renewintl.org).

Faith-Sharing Principles and Guidelines

The following guidelines will keep your faith-sharing community focused and help you to grow in faith, hope, and love.

Principles

— Faith is a gift from God. God leads each person on his or her spiritual journey. This happens in the context of the Christian community.

— Christ, the Word made flesh, is the root and foundation of Christian faith. It is because of Christ, and in and through him, that we come together to share our faith.

— "Faith sharing" refers to the shared reflections on the action of God in one's life experience as related to Scripture and the faith of the Church.

— Faith sharing is not discussion, problem solving, nor Scripture study. It is an opportunity for an encounter between a person in the concrete circumstances of his or her own life and a loving God, leading to a conversion of heart.

— The entire faith-sharing process is an expression of prayerful reflection.

Guidelines

— Constant attention to respect, honesty, and openness for each person will assist the community's growth.

— Each person shares on the level where he or she feels comfortable.

— Silence is a vital part of the total process. Participants are given time to reflect before any sharing begins, and a period of comfortable silence might occur between sharing by individual participants.

— Before sharing a second time, participants are encouraged to wait until all others who wish to do so have contributed.

— The entire community is responsible for participating and faith sharing.

— Confidentiality, allowing each person to share honestly, is essential.

— The natural culmination of the sharing should be the action commitment, the key to the spiritual growth of both individuals and community.

Structure and Flow of a Session

On pages xiii-xx, we presented some of the key elements that should be present for good, healthy faith sharing. We also talked about the importance of balance. Here is another way of looking at a session, paying attention to the way it should be structured so that there is a natural flow, one part leading the participants to the next, deeper stage.

Having a structured routine frees the group from having to figure out "What do we do next?" It allows the members to concentrate on the what, rather than the how, to pay more attention to their inner selves and to the Word of God.

If you follow the suggested timings, a session will last 90 minutes.

Gather (Step 1) *[15 minutes]*

Elements

- Introductions [First time only]
- Focus for the Session
- Opening Prayer and Opening Song [5 minutes]
- Living Our Faith (begins with Session 2) [10 minutes]

Purpose

- This is a sacred time. We enter it deliberately, as a community that has chosen to faith share together.
- We greet each other, we become aware that we are in the presence of God, and we pray for the grace to grow in faith.
- We share how the previous session has influenced our lives since we last met.
- We focus on the theme of the session that is about to unfold.

Reflection (Step 2) *[55 minutes]*

Elements

- See (opening story)
- Scripture reading
- Invitation to reflect on the Scripture [10 minutes]
- Reflection
- Invitation to Share (a question, or two) [10 minutes]

Purpose

- This part is about how the theme of the session relates to your life.
- After listening to a short reflection, everyone has the opportunity – helped by the questions—to reflect upon and share something of his or her own experience.

Invitation to Act (Step 3) *[20 minutes]*

Elements

- Commitment to an action, and suggestions for actions [15 minutes]
- Closing prayer [5 minutes]

Purpose

This part prompts the participants to understand that faith and faith sharing should impel us to commit to a specific and concrete act in the coming week, an act which flows from the sharing. This may be either a personal or a group action. Above all, it should be an action that, while challenging, is eminently doable.

Examples, linked to the theme of the reflection, are offered in this book. These are secondary to actions that the group members themselves discern as the fruit of their sharing.

The faith-sharing session concludes—as it began—in prayer.

"We have forgotten that we ourselves are dust of the earth; our very bodies are made up of her elements, we breathe her air and we receive life and refreshment from her waters."

Pope Francis, *Laudato Si'*, 2

SESSION 1

Our Relationship with God, with Each Other, and with the Earth

Focus for This Session

God made the world, "saw that it was good," and gave it to us to care for and share.

Suggested Environment

On a small table, which may be decorated with the color of the liturgical season, you may have a Bible, a burning candle, and a crucifix, in addition to articles representative of the environment, such as water, stones, soil, or plant life.

Gather

Introductions

Allow a few moments for participants to introduce themselves and briefly share how they became interested in joining Creation at the Crossroads.

Opening Prayer

Pray together:

Gracious, loving Creator God,
out of primeval darkness
you have flooded us with light.
You dispel the darkness of our minds and hearts,
and you guide our footsteps
as we try to follow your ways.
Be with us now as that light of truth.
Illumine our thoughts and conversations
with the light of your presence
as we gather together
with our sisters and brothers
to learn more about our relationship
with you, our God,
with each other, and with the earth,
our common home.
Amen.

Song Suggestion

"Morning Has Broken" (OCP)
Digital playlist is available at www.renewintl.org/creation

See: Lifelines Are All Connected

The impact of climate change on the most vulnerable populations is nowhere better illustrated than in Ethiopia, where increasing patterns of drought—one of the consequences of climate change—has a devastating ripple effect on the economy and on individual lives. When successive rainy seasons failed to materialize, in 2015 Catholic Relief Services (CRS) testified to the extent of the crisis: the numbers of people seeking emergency food assistance nearly doubled in the course of one year from around 4.5 million to about 8.2 million. Tens of millions more are affected in the Horn of Africa, which includes Kenya, Somalia, Sudan, and South Sudan.

This debacle in Ethiopia provides a good example of how interconnected every element of the environment is. For example, the drought wiped out the plant life that livestock normally graze on. As a result herding communities lost many animals and can demand only meager prices for the emaciated animals that survived. Loss of crops means loss of seeds, and farmers left with no alternatives often resort to eating the seeds that they would have planted for the next season. The combination of crop failures and loss of income led inevitably to malnutrition, a particular problem for hundreds of thousands of children, pregnant women, and nursing mothers.

CRS and its partners joined with the World Food Program and the government of Ethiopia in responding to the emergency. In addition to food relief, assistance from CRS involves helping farmers acquire seeds and livestock feed and, in partnership with the Church in Ethiopia, drilling for water sources that lie far below the surface of the earth.

Source: Catholic Relief Services, www.crs.org, October 26, 2015

The Word of God

Genesis 1:27-31
A World to Care For

Moment of Silent Reflection

In light of the impact of climate change in Ethiopia, what word, phrase, or image from the scripture reading touched your heart or spoke to your life?

Invitation to Share

1. Share the word, phrase, or image from the scripture reading that touched your heart.

2. What aspects of the created world do you personally find to be "very good"? Why?

Reflection

Pope Francis begins his encyclical *Laudato Si'* (*On Care for Our Common Home*) with words from the "Canticle of the Sun," composed by his namesake, St. Francis of Assisi: "Praise be to you my Lord, through our Sister, Mother Earth, who sustains and governs us, and who produces various fruits with colored flowers and herbs." The next line of the encyclical speaks to our own time: "This sister now cries out to us because of the harm we have inflicted on her by our irresponsible use and abuse of the goods with which God has endowed her." The challenge of protecting and caring for Mother Earth, our common home, is at the center of Pope Francis' message.

We humans are inflicting serious damage on our planet by exploiting its resources; polluting its water, air, and soil; and endangering its life-supporting systems. We are destroying the divine gift described by the author of the book of Genesis: valuable forests, wetlands, and other ecologically sensitive areas. We are killing off countless forms of life that took millions of years to evolve. Conservative estimates indicate that in the last quarter of the twentieth century ten percent of all living species became extinct. For these reasons Pope Francis in his encyclical calls upon all people of faith and good conscience to come together in dialogue about how this pattern of behavior can be reversed.

> "The urgent challenge to protect our common home includes a concern to bring the whole human family together to seek a sustainable and integral development ... The Creator does not abandon us; he never forsakes his loving plan or repents of having created us. Humanity still has the ability to work together in building our common home. ... I urgently appeal, then, for a new dialogue about how we are shaping the future of our planet. We need a conversation which includes everyone, since the environmental challenge we are undergoing, and its human roots, concern and affect us all."
>
> Pope Francis, *Laudato Si'*, 13-14

To begin, we must understand what our faith teaches us about God, the Creator. When Christians celebrate Eucharist on Sunday, they profess the Nicene Creed, which begins "I believe in one God, the Father Almighty, maker of heaven and earth, of all things visible and invisible...." These words are based on the accounts of creation in the Book of Genesis: God divides his work into three days of separation (light/darkness, heaven/earth, waters above/waters below). This is followed by three days of decoration (sun, moon, stars, birds, fish, and all living creatures). After each stage, the harmony, order, and beauty of the earth is punctuated by the words "God saw how good it was!"

On the sixth day of creation, Scripture tells us in a symbolic narrative, "God created man in his image; in the divine image he created him; male and female he created them. And God looked at everything he had made and he found it very good." In the ancient world, "image" was used to represent the king's presence where he could not be in person. When applied to the Genesis text that means that to be created in the "image of God" is to be God's representative on the earth.

Every human being, created out of love, made in God's image, has an immense dignity. We are capable of self-knowledge, self-giving, and of entering into communion with other persons. Each of us is the result of the thought of God; each of us is willed and loved by God; each of us is necessary. We have been chosen to be partners in the dialogue of creation, worthy caretakers of that which is meant by God to exist in harmony, good order, and right relationships. We've been fashioned as relational beings who can't exist without other relational beings. We share a world of nature on which we depend for air, water, and food—life itself. The wisdom of the Scriptures suggests that human life is grounded in three fundamental and closely intertwined relationships: with God, with our neighbor, and with the earth itself. And, we are part of a larger community of life which God recognized as "very good" at the end of the first creation story (Gn 1:31).

Harmony and right relationship are beautiful concepts, but we human beings don't always do our part to make them real. Most often we fail because in some way we act as if we were gods—not caring for the environment like a loving family who work together to maintain a shared household, but treating the natural world as though it existed for our benefit alone.

Some have failed to understand this truth because they misinterpret the words of God in Genesis: "Be fertile and multiply, fill the earth and subdue it. Have dominion over the birds of the air, the fish of the sea, and all living things that move on the earth." To "subdue the earth" does not mean to destroy or exploit it. The nuance of the verb, as it is used in Genesis, is to control. Human beings must work the land in order to gain our sustenance, but we must do it responsibly! The phrase "having dominion over the earth" is not a license for tyranny; we can't do with the earth whatever we like. We are called by God to exercise the real power that we have in the manner of Christ—in loving service to God and neighbor. Being given dominion is a challenge to be accountable for the care of the earth as a sacred trust. We must continue developing and improving upon it. Our efforts at re-working and shaping the earth are intended to make the result "good," just as God made it in the beginning.

A way of understanding the partnership between God and humankind is found in Genesis 2:15: "God then took man and settled him in the Garden of Eden to cultivate and care for it." In other words, we can take from the land whatever is needed for our sustenance, but we must be sure to protect it and give it proper oversight, not only for ourselves but also for future generations. We don't "own" the earth; it is given to us in trusteeship to be used for the common good. These ancient stories, full of symbolism, bear witness to a conviction that we today share, that everything is interconnected. Genuine care for our lives, our relationships with other human beings and with nature are inseparable from fraternity, justice, and faithfulness to others.

The Hebrew Scriptures—especially the Psalms, the prophets, and wisdom literature—repeat in many different ways that God's love is the fundamental moving force in all created things. Each creature, no matter how large or small, from the grasshopper to the elephant, from the little minnow to the orca whale, has its own purpose. No one, no creature, is superfluous. The entire universe speaks of God's love for all of us creatures, living and non-living: soil, water, mountains, forests, Arctic tundra. Everything is like a caress of God. It speaks of God's presence.

Biblical wisdom about relationships and the inter-connection of all creation helps us to understand the frequent references by Pope Francis to "integral ecology." Ecology is a combination of the Greek words *oikos*, meaning home, and *logos* meaning a teaching. Ecology then is the study of how organisms interact with one another and with their common home. "Integral" adds an element of completeness: humans and all creatures of land, sea, and air, and our environment, are intimately connected as parts of a whole. Harming or destroying one part of the whole will cause harm and negative repercussions for another part. If we pollute our streams and rivers, we endanger the lives of the creatures that live in the water and the wellbeing of people who live along the banks. All of us are linked by unseen bonds, and together we form a universal family, sharing a common home.

Invitation to Share

Take a few moments of silence to reflect on the following questions. Then share your reflections.

1. Scripture teaches over and over that Creation is good. Share an experience in your life that has taught this to you.

2. Before Pope Francis' encyclical, had you ever heard about the Church's teachings on care for the environment? When and where? What was your initial reaction to this?

3. What relationship do you see between religious faith and care for the environment?

Invitation to Act

Being together and sharing in a small Christian community fosters growth in our faith and in our spirituality. However, no communal sharing is complete without a serious commitment to putting our faith into practice. In this session we have reflected on our duty to preserve our common home as the "good" natural world that God created. How does this inspire us to act? The following are examples.

1. Spend time outdoors in prayer in a favorite spot. At your small group's next meeting, be prepared to share what that experience was like for you and what you learned.

2. Research has shown that we make our biggest environmental impact through our transportation, food choices, and the energy we use to power our homes. With our diets, the amount of meat we eat creates the greatest negative impact on God's creation because meat production uses such enormous amounts of water and energy. Make a commitment to eat meat at one less meal per week in the coming month.

3. Take a trip to a local community that is experiencing environmental degradation. For example, a community near a power plant, industrial waste site, or landfill. What can you do to lift up their concerns and protect their health?

4. Research the changes in biodiversity in your region. Which species are declining in populations? What can you do to help protect the habitats of the wildlife species in your area?

5. As a group, survey your community and select a public area that has been littered or otherwise uncared for. Create a plan to improve and maintain this area.

6. Do research on consumer products that are made from materials derived from endangered life forms, including elephants, rhinos, and sea turtles. Consider how this information may affect your own shopping choices and help raise others' awareness of this problem.

7. Research the impact of garden and lawn pesticides that can harm wildlife, and find alternative means of maintaining your own property. If you live in a condominium community, ask your owners association to discuss this with the landscaping contractor.

8. Find out how nature areas and wildlife habitats, as well as parks, farmland, historic sites, and flood-prone lands are preserved in your municipality. Then participate in the process to have that land protected from development.

Closing Prayer

Divide the group in two and alternately offer these praises:

Group 1:   Glory be to you, O generous Creator God,
for the earth, sea, and sky.

Group 2:   Glory be to you for blessing us
with the wondrous array of birds of the air,
fish of the sea, and the remarkable diversity
of all living creatures.

Group 1:   Glory be to you for household pets
that give us such joy with their faithful presence.

Group 2:   Glory be to you for our families and loved ones
who support and sustain us.

Group 1:   Glory be to you for our church communities
who remind us of your presence.

Group 2:   Glory and thanks to you for bringing us together
to reflect on the importance of the earth, our common home.

Pause to allow individual members to give glory to God for some gift or blessing.

All: **May our time spent together honor your name and
bring us joy, hope, and peace. Amen.**

Looking Ahead

Prepare for the next session by prayerfully reading

— Session 2, "Water: A Basic and Inalienable Right"

— Isaiah 35:1-8

— Pope Francis' encyclical *Laudato Si'*, paragraphs 1-31.

If you have not yet read the Introduction to *Creation at the Crossroads,* be sure to read it before your group's second meeting. It contains important information about the Catholic Church's teaching on the environment.

Learn More

Pope Benedict's XVI's books, *The Environment* (Our Sunday Visitor) and *10 Commandments for the Environment* (Ave Maria Press).

GreenFaith offered two webinars to introduce the encyclical to the public. One featured Catholic responses, moderated by Fr. Tom Reese, SJ, of *America* Magazine; another featured Muslim, Hindu, Jewish, and Protestant responses. **http://www.greenfaith.org/ success-stories/religious-teachings-webinars-march-2015**

"The Theologians Respond: *Laudato Si'*." Sponsored by America Media, experts in Catholic social teaching offer an overview of the content and significance of the teachings in the text, as well as background on Catholic engagement on social issues and discuss the possible impact of this text on national and international politics. **https://www.youtube.com/watch?v=EdAJO-anDmY**

"Access to safe drinkable water is a basic and universal human right, since it is essential to human survival and, as such, is a condition for the exercise of other human rights."

Pope Francis, *Laudato Si'*, 30

SESSION 2

Water: A Basic and Inalienable Right

Focus for This Session

Access to clean water, an essential gift from God, is a human right.

Suggested Environment

On a small table, which may be decorated with the color of the liturgical season, you may have a Bible, a burning candle, and a crucifix, in addition to articles representative of the environment, such as water, stones, soil, or plant life.

Gather

Opening Prayer

Pray together:

Gracious, loving Creator God,
you who have brought living creatures from primeval waters,
and have sustained these various forms of creation with food and water.
We thank you for the presence of your Son, Jesus Christ,
who has graced our lives with the waters of baptism
and the gifts of the Holy Spirit, and sustained all life
through the waters of the earth.

Awaken and bring to life the seeds of your wisdom,
touch our minds and hearts,
that we may be open and receptive
to the teaching of this session.
We ask this in the power of your name. Amen.

Song Suggestion

"Come to the Water" (OCP)
Digital playlist is available at www.renewintl.org/creation

Living Our Faith

Share briefly your experience of putting into effect the action you chose after the last session.

See: Millions Lack Clean Water

In some parts of the world, folks don't give clean water a second thought. But not everywhere: estimates vary, but the evidence is that more than 700 million people do not have access to clean water, and almost 2.5 billion don't have access to adequate sanitation. The result is millions of deaths each year due to water-borne diseases.

It's a big problem, but not so big that one person can't make a dent in it. One example is Rosemary Breen of Brisbane, Australia, who has taken an interest in villages in Myanmar where clean water is scarce, and she has inspired others to take action to resolve the problem.

In 2014, for example, she invited Laura Daley of Inverell, New South Wales, Australia, to tour villages in Myanmar where 40 water tanks had been built through financing organized by Rosemary. Her goal is 100 tanks.

The 40 tanks serve nearly 8500 people in villages and schools, people who previously may have traveled great distances to acquire water that had a high salt content or drew contaminated water from a local lake.

Meeting the villagers and seeing their living conditions prompted Laura Daley to provide a village with a tank herself and take a permanent interest in the issue.

"I didn't have a true understanding of the impact until I really saw it for myself," Laura said. "I think it's just a basic life essential; water is the basis of life and everyone should have the opportunity to have access to clean water."

Source: The Inverell Times, March 11, 2014

The Word of God

Isaiah 35: 1-8
"Waters shall break forth in the wilderness"

Moment of Silent Reflection

In light of the work of women like Rosemary and Laura to bring water to the people of Myanmar, what word, phrase, or image from the scripture reading touched your heart or spoke to your life?

Invitation to Share

1. Share the word, phrase, or image from the scripture reading that touched your heart.

2. A large part of the human family lives without the kind of abundance described in Isaiah's prophecy. In what way do you feel that your Christian faith calls on you to play a part in the fulfillment of God's promise in that passage?

Reflection

Pope Francis is concerned about the unsustainable level of consumption of finite natural resources. With respect to one vital resource, he writes, "Fresh drinking water is an issue of primary importance, since it is indispensable for human life and for supporting terrestrial and aquatic systems" (*Laudato Si'*, 28).

Though an increasing number of people are experiencing water shortages, those who are poor suffer most. Seven hundred fifty million people do not have access to clean water; 2.4 billion people do not have adequate sanitation. And yet, this resource continues to be wasted and poorly managed in the developed and developing worlds.

Agriculture, industry, and the health of people and eco-systems depend on water. More people die annually from exposure to unsafe water than from all forms of violence, including war. Children are especially susceptible to water-borne disease. Forty-five thousand children (one child every 20 seconds) die every day from preventable water-borne diseases (U.N. Fact Sheet on Water and Sanitation).

In many places, water sources are threatened by the pollution produced by inadequate sewage treatment and mining, farming, and industrial practices. This is especially true in countries and municipalities lacking regulations and controls. Every day, two million tons of sewage and industrial and agricultural waste are dumped into the world's waters. Detergents and chemical products used in households throughout the world also frequently end up in rivers, lakes, and streams.

At the same time that water pollution is growing, the demand for water is increasing. In addition to the needs of a growing population, some countries are experiencing a rise in the standard of living within some segments of society. For example, Christiana Peppard, in her book *Just Water,* shows the relationship between the increased demand for water and the growth of the middle class in China and India. Those in the middle class are more educated and have higher incomes. The increased income is changing their eating habits. Diets which once consisted of vegetables and chicken or fish now regularly include beef dinners. To produce a pound of beef requires 1,799 gallons of water. Producing a pound of chicken requires 460 gallons of water.

Modern technology has also increased water usage at a massive scale. Producing one micro-chip requires roughly 32 gallons of water. That may not seem like much compared to a pound of beef. However, by 2013 there were nearly as many cell phones in the world (6.8 billion) as there were people. Imagine the amount of water involved.

Pope Francis writes, "Some studies warn that an acute water shortage may occur within a few decades unless urgent action is taken. The environmental repercussions could affect billions of people; it is also conceivable that the control of water by large multinational businesses may become a major source of conflict in this century" (*Laudato Si',* 31). The United Nations states, "By 2025, 1.8 billion people will be living in countries or regions with absolute water scarcity, and two thirds of the world population could be under stress conditions" (U.N. Food and Agricultural Organization).

Pope Francis is especially concerned about the movement toward privatizing water. "Even as the quality of available water is constantly diminishing, in some places there is a growing tendency, despite its scarcity, to privatize this resource, turning it into a commodity, subject to the laws of the market" (*Laudato Si',* 30). On July 28, 2010, The United Nations passed a resolution recognizing the human right to water and sanitation and acknowledging that clean drinking water and sanitation are essential to the realization of all human rights. Pope Francis affirms this position, writing that "access to safe drinkable water is a basic and universal human right, since it is essential to human survival and, as such, is a condition for the exercise of other human rights" (*Laudato Si',* 30). Access to water is a "right-to-life" issue.

Privatization of water as a commodity to be sold for profit is especially harmful to those who are poor, who often cannot pay a high price for water, even when it is accessible. Bottled water is a daily reminder of the privatization of water. Multinational corporations bottle it in plastic, market it cleverly, and stock supermarket and convenience-store shelves, charging a thousand or more times the cost of tap water. The water can come from clean natural sources, but most of it simply comes from faucets. Ironically, the largest consuming country of bottled water is the United States, where tap water is almost universally available, is inexpensive, and is perfectly clean for consumption.

Earth is called the water, or blue, planet. Here are some significant facts:

- All of life is dependent upon water.

- Over 70 percent of the earth is covered by water.

- 97.5 percent of the earth's water is salt water.

- 2.5 percent is fresh water, much of which is locked in ice caps and Polar Regions.

- The amount of water on the earth has not changed for three billion years. There is no known practical way to manufacture water; water can only be recycled and reused.

- The mature human body is 70 percent water. The physical composition of all living things—from pine trees to puppies to pansies—is primarily water.

- We came from water and are sustained by water.

In this interconnected world in which plastic is produced from oil, it is significant to note that making plastic bottles to meet Americans' demand for bottled water annually, requires more than 17 million barrels of oil, enough fuel for more than one million cars a year. The process also generates more than 2.5 million tons of carbon dioxide (Corporate Accountability International).

The increased scarcity of water will relate to every aspect of life. The availability and cost of food, for example, will affect billions of people. "It is also conceivable that the control of water by large multinational companies may become a major source of conflict in this century," Pope Francis warns us (*Laudato Si'*, 31).

Water is the natural resource most frequently referred to in the Bible— more than 500 times. The semi-arid environment of the biblical world is a partial explanation for this frequency. However, the connection between water and life is a theme that threads its way through both the Old and New Testaments and in religious literature all over the world. The scripture passage for today's session, Isaiah 35:1-8, speaks of the regenerating and life-giving aspects of water in the desert. The streams bursting forth in the desert and the burning sands transformed into pools of water are symbols of new beginnings. Such signs will accompany those on the "highway called the holy way." The abundance of flowers, the new strength received by the weak and feeble, the healing of the blind and the deaf, the thirsty ground springing into new watery life are all indicators of a new age. To those who are forlorn, discouraged, and looking forward to a "new creation," these signs foreshadow the presence once again of the Creator God, the source of life.

The world's major religions all reverence water for its cleansing and life-sustaining qualities. In the gospel story (Jn 4:1-42), the well, the water jar, and the woman herself who, like her neighbors, must draw from the well every day in order to live, all symbolize the indispensable role of water. In the Catholic tradition, water is significant as a sign or symbol, especially in the sacrament of baptism. At the Easter Vigil, water is blessed in larger quantities and used throughout the year for holy water fonts and for the celebration of baptism. At the Easter vigil, adults who have been prepared for entry into the Christian community are often baptized by immersion and welcomed by the entire parish community. The waters of baptism, followed by the sacraments of confirmation and Eucharist, are the ritual signs of transformation into the new life in Christ. The words and gestures of this rite of acceptance give full meaning to the words of Jesus, "Whoever drinks the water I shall give, will never thirst; the water I shall give shall become in him a spring of water welling up to eternal life" (Jn 4:14-15).

> **"Our world has a grave social debt towards the poor who lack access to drinking water, because they are denied the right to a life consistent with their inalienable dignity. This debt can be paid partly by an increase in funding to provide clean water and sanitary services among the poor. But water continues to be wasted, not only in the developed world but in developing countries which possess it in abundance. This shows that the problem of water is partly an education and cultural issue, since there is little awareness of the seriousness of such behavior in a context of great inequality."**
>
> Pope Francis, *Laudato Si'*, 30

Pope Francis, in speaking of the material universe as an expression of God's love and boundless affection for us, describes water as a "caress of God." We are called through awareness, education, and commitment to protect this precious and limited resource. May we pass on this expression of God's love to future generations.

Invitation to Share

Take a few moments of silence to reflect on the following questions. Then share your reflections.

1. What habits and attitudes can you develop with regard to your use of water?

2. How do you understand the opinion that "access to clean water is a right-to-life issue"?

3. How do water shortages affect the poor and vulnerable?

4. What are the advantages and disadvantages of using bottled water?

Invitation to Act

Being together and sharing in a small Christian community fosters growth in our faith and in our spirituality. However, no communal sharing is complete without a serious commitment to putting our faith into practice. In this session we have reflected on the vital role of water for all forms of life. How does this inspire us to act? The following are examples.

1. Research the source of drinking water in your area: Where does your water come from? How is it filtered or treated? Do you know where it goes when it leaves your house?

2. Make a list of those activities at home in which you could conserve water.

3. Millions of people lack access to clean water, and more than a billion lack access to sanitation facilities. Organizations such as Catholic Relief Services fund projects to provide access to clean water and sanitation. Begin a campaign in your parish to raise funds to support such a project.

Closing Prayer

Pray together:

Gracious, loving Creator God,
thank you for the gift of water that gives us life,
quenches our thirst, and sustains our farmlands and gardens.

You bless us with streams, rivers, and oceans
to feed us, refresh us, and enthrall us with the bounty of aquatic life.

Give us the wisdom to appreciate that water is a precious gift,
not a commodity.

Pardon us for our failures in not using the gift of water properly.

May we retain and act on what we have learned from this session
and pass it on to future generations. Amen.

Looking Ahead

Prepare for the next session by prayerfully reading

— Session 3, "Global Climate Change"

— Hosea 4:1-3

— Pope Francis' encyclical *Laudato Si'*, paragraphs 32-47.

Learn More

Just Water, Theology, Ethics, and the Global Water Crisis by
Christiana Peppard; Orbis, 2014.

GreenFaith's Water Shield Program offers parishes and faith
communities a weekend-long program to reduce their water use and
to equip their members to do the same:
http://www.greenfaith.org/programs/greenfaith-shield

"Climate change is a global problem with grave implications…. It represents one of the principal challenges facing humanity today. Its worst impact will probably be felt by developing countries in coming decades."

Pope Francis, *Laudato Si'*, 25

SESSION 3

Global Climate Change

Focus for This Session

Climate change impacts everyone, and most drastically those who are poor.

Suggested Environment

On a small table, which may be decorated with the color of the liturgical season, you may have a Bible, a burning candle, and a crucifix, in addition to articles representative of the environment, such as water, stones, soil, or plant life.

Gather

Opening Prayer

Pray together:

Gracious, loving Creator God,
we thank you and praise you again
for the wondrous gifts of creation.
You have blessed us with the power and beauty
of mighty mountains and golden plains,
the vastness of your star-filled heavens
and the mysterious depth of the seas.

They blend and weave together
with such effortless harmony and give us joy.
We humans too are a part of it: your majestic handiwork.
When we allow ourselves the time and space to absorb it all,
we can only say, "Thank you."
But there also have been times
when we were too busy to look heavenwards.
We focused too much on ourselves; we had eyes but did not see.
We disrespected what you had created.
Be with us today as we gather together.
Fill us with your mighty Spirit to recognize
what we should have seen, but did not.
Show us the way to be wise caretakers
of this precious world that we call our common home. Amen.

Song Suggestion

"Amazing Grace" (OCP)
Digital playlist available at www.renewintl.org/creation

Living Our Faith

Share briefly your experience of putting into effect the action you chose after the last session.

See: The Sea May Swallow a Nation

The image of a nation disappearing from the planet was once the stuff of science fiction. Now it is a real prospect in the foreseeable future for the Maldives, an archipelago in the Indian Ocean.

Because of rising sea levels, the result of global warming, environmental studies have projected that the whole nation could be under water by the end of the century. A United Nations panel on climate change has warned that most of the 200 inhabited islands in the Maldives might have to be abandoned, and their residents turned into refugees, by 2100.

The Maldives constitute the smallest nation in Asia with a population of less than 400,000 people spread over about 35,000 square miles. The average elevation is only 4 feet 11 inches above sea level, and the highest natural point in the country is only 7 feet 10 inches. The same UN panel has predicted that sea levels globally will rise on average by from 1 to 3 feet by the end of the century, with the higher end of that range more likely.

The government of the Maldives has pledged to make the country carbon-neutral by 2019; the government knows that that action in itself will not save the Maldives but is an acknowledgement that countries all over the world must make such commitments if the warming of the atmosphere and the loss of ice sheets and glaciers is to be stemmed by a sharp reduction in the use of fossil fuels.

The Maldives are hardly in this alone. An analysis by Climate Central estimated that people in all parts of the world face increased risk of regular flooding by the end of the century: more than a quarter of the population of Vietnam—23 million people; about 50 million people in China; more than 2.5 million people in the United Kingdom; and about 3.1 million people in the United States, and hundreds of millions of people in other countries.

The Word of God

Hosea 4:1-3
Beasts, Birds, and Fish Perish

Moment of Silent Reflection

Given the plight of the Maldives Islands, what word, phrase or image from the scripture reading touched your heart or spoke to your life?

Invitation to Share

1. Share the word, phrase, or image from the scripture reading that touched your heart.

2. The people of Israel are judged by God's prophet, Hosea, for not abiding by the laws of covenant love. Even the earth suffers because of their neglect. As you go about your everyday activities, how conscious are you of God's love for everything he has created? How does your answer affect your behavior?

Reflection

Global climate change is a very good example of how all created reality on the earth is inter-connected. The earth is a complex of living systems, or a system of systems. Global climate change threatens the interdependence of all systems of life. Overwhelming scientific evidence drives home one central point: the fate of the earth and the fate of humans are one. What makes this an issue of major concern is that climate change poses the greatest threat to life on the earth that we have ever faced. Unless we confront this issue and deal with it soon, it will impact not only us but future generations as well.

In the scriptural passage taken from the prophecy of Hosea, the scene is a legal proceeding taking place at the city gate. The people of Israel are summoned before the judge and indicted with a listing of violations of the covenant. The verdict is "guilty" as charged. When the covenant is broken, the object of the covenant, the land, is no longer secure and fertile. The land returns to being a desert, its past unredeemed condition. The indictment of the people Israel impacts even the earth and its creatures: "the beasts of the field, the birds of the air, and even the fish of the sea perish."

These words are not unlike those of Pope Francis: "Carbon dioxide pollution increases the acidification of the oceans and compromises the marine food chain. If present trends continue, this century may well witness extraordinary climate change and an unprecedented destruction of ecosystems, with serious consequences for all of us" (*Laudato Si'*, 24).

A solid consensus among climate scientists throughout the world indicates a disturbing warming of the climatic system. Average temperatures are climbing steadily and dangerously, as recent experiments have shown. This warming is accompanied by a constant rise in sea levels, mainly from the melting of glaciers and mountain ice caps. When oceans get too warm they cause fiercer storms, more frequent hurricanes,

> **"The human environment and the natural environment deteriorate together; we cannot adequately combat environmental degradation unless we attend to causes related to human and social degradation. In fact, the deterioration of the environment and of society affects the most vulnerable people on the planet: ... For example, the depletion of fishing reserves especially hurts small fishing communities without the means to replace those resources; water pollution particularly affects the poor who cannot buy bottled water; and rises in the sea level mainly affect impoverished coastal populations who have nowhere else to go. The impact of present imbalances is also seen in the premature death of many of the poor, in conflicts sparked by the shortage of resources, and in any number of other problems which are insufficiently represented on global agendas."**
>
> Pope Francis, *Laudato Si'*, 27

and other extreme weather events. Scientific studies also indicate that most global warming in recent decades is attributable to a great concentration of greenhouse gases. Gases such as carbon dioxide, methane, and nitrogen oxide are released into the atmosphere, mainly as a result of human activity, from sources that include cars, buses, factories, and coal-burning electrical plants. Almost 56 percent of the total share of global emissions from carbon dioxide comes from the use of fossil fuels. These emissions trap the energy that emanates from the sun and is reflected by the earth. The gases, which then can't escape into space, produce what is called the "greenhouse effect." Climate scientists are concerned that we will soon reach a dangerous tipping point at which global weather changes become irreversible and trigger further global warming.

Climate change is real, and it's getting worse. Pope Francis does not mince words: "Climate change is a global problem with grave implications: environmental, social, economic, political, and (one that impacts) the distribution of goods. It represents one of the principal challenges facing humanity in our day" (*Laudato Si'*, 25). While the words of the prophet Hosea represent a vastly different time, culture, and religious context, the judgment that even "the beasts of the field and birds of the air" suffer the effects of human failure is worthy of reflection (Hosea 4:3).

Global warming has far-reaching implications. In the United States alone, one of the more striking examples of climate change has been the frequency and intensity of storms and heavy downpours in the Midwest, severe droughts in the West, and flooding where it is not normally expected. On a broader, global scale, warming effects appear in the loss of Arctic summer sea ice, the melting of Greenland's ice sheet, an increase in El Niño events, severe changes in boreal forest ecosystems, declining fish yields, and—as we've already seen—absorption of more carbon dioxide in oceans, causing acidity and impacting the food chain. All of creation is interconnected. The earth, our common home, is a system of systems. We impact one another for good or ill.

Climate change disproportionately affects the poor. Many of the poor live in areas particularly affected by phenomena related to warming. Their subsistence is largely dependent on natural reserves and eco-systemic services such as agriculture, fishing, and forestry. They have no other resources to fall back on. Their access to social services and other protections is limited. For example, when climate change impacts their livelihood of farming, fishing, or hunting, they are forced to leave their homes and migrate elsewhere. Of all of the effects of climate change, the plight of displaced people is particularly alarming. They are not recognized by officialdom as refugees but as migrants. As we have witnessed in the political upheaval in the Middle East, refugees suffer the loss of a livelihood they are left behind without enjoying any legal protection. Once again, these are instances of "systemic change" in which, beginning with drought, flooding, or very often with war, the lives of innocent, poor people are impacted dramatically. This environmental inequality creates a strange economic phenomenon. Poor countries are often financially indebted to rich countries because of environmental crises caused by those same affluent nations.

While personal responsibility is an important step toward reversing climate change, political, economic, and structural transformations are needed if the reform is to be sufficient and sustainable. As citizens and beneficiaries of planet Earth, we are in this together. Pope Francis, quoting the encyclical *Centesimus Annus* by Pope St. John Paul II, goes on to say, "Every effort to protect and improve our world entails profound changes in 'lifestyles, models of production and consumption, and the established structures of power which today govern societies.'" Some people argue that Pope Francis should stay out of climate change debates and "leave it to the scientists." But Francis and the Church know that protecting creation is first and foremost a religious and moral issue. The pope speaks not as a scientist but as a global pastoral leader. He does not point fingers at anyone but tries to awaken minds, hearts, and consciences of all people of good will to enter into a much-needed dialogue about the fate of our common home.

Invitation to Share

Take a few moments of silence to reflect on the following questions. Then share your reflections.

1. Give a personal example of how you have experienced global climate change.

2. The poor and vulnerable are disproportionately affected by environmental degradation. How is climate change affecting the poor and vulnerable now?

3. Explain how and why the issue of global climate change is a moral issue.

4. Why should people of faith be concerned about global climate change?

Invitation to Act

Being together and sharing in a small Christian community fosters growth in our faith and in our spirituality. However, no communal sharing is complete without a serious commitment to putting our faith into practice. In this session we have reflected on global climate change. How does this inspire us to act? The following are examples.

1. Consult with your local utility or public utilities commission on having an "energy audit" of your own home. In a journal or notebook, jot down what steps you might take in conserving energy at home.

2. Some power companies conduct energy audits and recommend corrective measures for their customers. Contact your power company to see if they offer such a service.

3. The carbon footprint is a very powerful tool to understand the impact of personal behavior on global warming. Calculate your or your family's carbon footprint, which is the amount of carbon dioxide your activities create (http://www3.epa.gov/carbon-footprint-calculator/). In a journal or notebook, jot down what steps you and your family can take to reduce your carbon footprint.

Closing Prayer

Beginning with the leader, members of the group pray in turn:

Leader:	Gracious and loving Creator God, you have reminded us once again in today's sharing of our call to protect the earth.
Reader 1:	Each of us is different, having different personal gifts, though sharing the same Spirit.
Reader 2:	Teach us to keep our minds and hearts open to the promptings of your Spirit, that we may learn how to use our gifts, each in our own way and together.
Reader 3:	Show us how we can be effective caretakers of this good earth.
Reader 4:	May we do what we can to make this a healthier and better world for those who will come after us.
All:	**We ask this in the name of your Son, Jesus Christ. Amen.**

Looking Ahead

Prepare for the next session by prayerfully reading

— Session 4, "The Cry of the Earth Becomes the Cry of the Poor"

— Luke 6:20-26

— Pope Francis' encyclical *Laudato Si'*, paragraphs 48-61.

Learn More

Visit the Catholic Climate Covenant's website,
www.catholicclimatecovenant.org and GreenFaith's website,
www.greenfaith.org, to learn about what Catholic and interfaith
organizations are doing about climate change.

"The New Paradigm of Catholic Energy Ethics," guest blog by
Erin Lothes Biviano, **http://catholicmoraltheology.com/
a-new-paradigm-for-catholic-energy-ethics/**

Database of State Incentives for Renewables & Efficiency,
http://www.dsireusa.org/

Environmental Protection Agency: Residential Energy Efficiency,
**http://www3.epa.gov/statelocalclimate/local/topics/
residential.html**

"We have to realize that a true ecological approach always becomes a social approach; it must integrate questions of justice in debates on the environment, so as to hear both the cry of the earth and the cry of the poor."

Pope Francis, *Laudato Si'*, 49

SESSION 4

The Cry of the Earth Becomes the Cry of the Poor

Focus for This Session

Poor and vulnerable people and communities suffer from damage to the environment.

Suggested Environment

On a small table, which may be decorated with the color of the liturgical season, you may have a Bible, a burning candle, and a crucifix, in addition to articles representative of the environment, such as water, stones, soil, or plant life.

Gather

Opening Prayer

Pray together:

O God, who are the Ground of all Being and Source of Life,
you have blessed us generously with the gifts of creation:
air to breathe, food to eat, and water to drink.

We thank you in a special way for the gift of your Son,
our Lord Jesus Christ, for the blessings of our families,
friends, and loved ones, who sustain us with life and love.

We pray with gratitude and also with deep awareness
of our brothers and sisters throughout the world
who lack the blessings and gifts we take for granted.

Make us more aware and appreciative of our blessings,
and willing to contribute to a more just and equitable sharing
of the gifts of creation, especially with those who are in need.

We ask this in the name of our Savior, Jesus Christ. Amen.

Song Suggestion

"The Cry of the Poor" (OCP)
Digital playlist available at www.renewintl.org/creation

Living Our Faith

Share briefly your experience of putting into effect the action you chose after the last session.

See: Greed Quenched a Heroic Life

Sister Dorothy Stang, SND, was an American missionary nun, who grew up in Dayton, Ohio. She joined the Sisters of Notre Dame de Namur at age 17. In 1966, she left for the city of Coroatá in Brazil where her first assignment was to educate local farmers who had no formal schooling. The main threat to the Amazon region at that time came from large-scale ranchers who ruthlessly drove farmers from their lands. Small farms and forested areas were cleared by burning and then planted again with crops used to produce bio-fuels. Very often the powerful ranchers, who displaced the poor from the land, paid the police and judges to look the other way.

Sister Dorothy was one of the few foreign missionaries in the area. She became a champion of farmers, indigenous groups, and the forest itself. She would camp outside of police stations and courthouses, demanding that the rights of her people be upheld. At one point, ranchers put a $50,000 bounty on her head. After leaving a particularly disagreeable meeting of ranchers and farmers, she was shot several times and killed, and her body was left alongside a muddy road. She was 73 years old, having served in Brazil for 39 years. The testimony of her life reminds us of the words of Jesus: "Blessed are you when people hate you, and exclude and insult you, and denounce your name as evil on account of the Son of Man. Rejoice and leap for joy on that day! Behold your reward will be great in heaven" (Luke 6: 22-23).

The Word of God

Luke 6:20-26
Your Reward is in Heaven

Moment of Silent Reflection

In light of the Sr. Dorothy's ministry in Brazil, what word, phrase, or image from the scripture reading touched your heart or spoke to your life?

Invitation to Share

1. Share the word, phrase, or image from the scripture reading that touched your heart.

2. How does this scripture passage bring you consolation? How does it challenge you?

Reflection

Poverty takes on new dimensions as unsustainably high use of natural resources leads to plunder and degradation of the natural environment. While all nations and all people are impacted, the poor suffer more than others, especially when their farms, forests, and subsistence-level livelihood stand in the way of what is called modern economic "progress." The gravest environmental effects are suffered by the poorest people. For example, the depletion of fishing resources due to over-fishing especially hurts small fishing communities that can't compete with large-scale corporate fishing operations. Water pollution, especially in Africa, affects the poor who cannot obtain fresh water easily or afford to buy bottled water. Rises in sea level mainly affect impoverished populations who do not have the resources to re-locate when their homes are threatened. The premature deaths of many poor people result from conflicts that arise when resources are not available. Agencies such as Catholic Relief Services that provide emergency relief and long-term development are working to ensure that the poorest and the most vulnerable are able to share in the basic needs of life. However, such assistance is limited and falls far short of the many needs throughout the world.

Pope Francis stresses the plight of the poor in his encyclical because Jesus teaches us to care for the poor and because poverty is a major issue throughout the world. The poor are often removed from centers of power and affluence. They need the Church to speak on their behalf, and they need empowerment so they can meet their needs and protect their families. In the developed world there is a lack of awareness of the problems that especially affect the poor and marginalized. Recent statistics indicate that almost three billion people of the world's population live on less than $2.50

per day. Even in the United States, one third of the population lives in households with perilously low incomes, according to U.S. Census Bureau statistics. Jesus spoke often of the needs of the poor, but in economic discussions in our times the problems of poor people are brought up almost as an afterthought, or some kind of "collateral damage." This geographical and intellectual distancing from the real-life experience of poverty leads in more prosperous people to a numbing of conscience and can invite a one-sided analysis that neglects major parts of society.

One of the more encouraging signs of our times is the number of secondary school and college students from developed countries who take part in social service experiences and study programs in Africa and elsewhere in the Southern Hemisphere. There is no better opportunity for a change of mind and heart than to be part of such an "immersion experience," to converse, interact, and share work opportunities with people of different cultures and economic levels. Pope Francis has praised such opportunities, which he refers to as "encounter experiences."

> "In different ways, developing countries, where the most important reserves in the biosphere are found, continue to fuel the development of richer countries at the cost of their own present and future. The land of the southern poor is rich and mostly unpolluted, yet access to ownership of goods and resources for meeting vital needs is inhibited by a system of commercial relations and ownership which is structurally perverse. The developed countries ought to help pay this debt by significantly limiting their consumption of non-renewable energy and by assisting poorer countries to support policies and programs of sustainable development."
>
> Pope Francis, *Laudato Si'*, 52

Another principle of justice and equity concerns the universal destiny of the goods of the earth. The world and its bounty have been created for the "good" of all human beings without exception. To live with dignity, every person is entitled to enough food to eat, clean water to drink, housing, and other basic human needs. It is painful to read the words of Pope Francis: "We know that approximately a third of all food produced is discarded, and 'whenever food is thrown out, it is as if it were stolen from the table of the poor.'" (*Laudato Si'*, 50). What an indictment! Today's scripture passage was quite direct: "Woe to you who are filled now, for you will be hungry."

As people created in the image and likeness of God, entitled to self-respect and dignity, we are also worthy of the basic sustenance of life. Assisting poor populations in acquiring the necessities of life is not merely a suggestion, it is a moral imperative.

Inequity affects not only individuals but entire countries. In view of this and taking into consideration environmental harm, it is necessary to consider an ethics of international relations, that may be referred to as an "ecological debt." If we are honest, we know that developed nations extract, use, and devour most of the natural resources of poorer, less-developed countries. After ceasing their activity and withdrawing, companies based in developed nations leave behind great human and environmental liabilities, including unemployment, abandoned towns, depletion of natural reserves, deforestation, and pollution stemming from open pits of mines still containing toxic materials. Pope Francis suggests that "developed countries ought to help pay this debt by significantly limiting their consumption of non-renewable energy and by assisting poorer countries to support policies and programs of sustainable development" (*Laudato Si'*, 52). Poorer countries are less capable of adopting new models for reducing environmental impact because they lack the financial resources to pay the costs.

Even in developed countries, the poor are at risk because of environmental degradation. For example, air pollution is responsible for 200,000 premature deaths annually in the United States, with most of those deaths striking people of color and poor people. The impact of pollution is not limited to developing countries but also plays out in societies across the world.

When addressing the issue of climate change in 2001, the United States Conference of Catholic Bishops said that greater attention must be given to the "needs of the poor, the weak and the vulnerable, in a debate more often dominated by more powerful interests" (*Global Climate Change: A Plea for Dialogue, Prudence, and the Common Good*). We need to strengthen the conviction that we are one human family. There are no frontiers or barriers, political or social, behind which we can hide. Still less is there room for what Pope Francis has called "the globalization of indifference." Caring for the poor of the world cannot be analyzed or explained in isolation. This demand of our faith must be seen within the context of a human community that is morally entitled to the basics of life.

Pope Francis wrote *Laudato Si'* to bring together men and women of faith and good conscience to read, reflect, deliberate, and act on the issues that can bring us together. Economics, politics, and technology alone cannot bring about a better, safer, healthier world. It is only people throughout the world, people who are concerned about the poor, people who are profoundly aware of how intimately we are connected with all human beings and with our environment that will help us repair our common home, where we can live together in security and peace.

Blessed are you who are poor, for the kingdom of God is yours.

Invitation to Share

Take a few moments of silence to reflect on the following questions. Then share your reflections.

1. The reflection describes the ways in which environmental degradation exacerbates poverty. What is your reaction to this?

2. What is your experience of the environment in which people who are poor live? How do you think their plight is relevant in your life and faith?

3. What is your reaction to the suggestion by Pope Francis that developed nations should recognize their "ecological debt" to undeveloped countries? Do you think that we as individuals living in developed nations have a similar "debt"?

Invitation to Act

Being together and sharing in a small Christian community fosters growth in our faith and in our spirituality. However, no communal sharing is complete without a serious commitment to putting our faith into practice. In this session we have reflected on how environmental damage disproportionately affects the poor and vulnerable. How does this inspire us to act? The following are examples.

1. Around the country, groups in many poor communities are coming together to fight pollution in their neighborhoods. Research whether there are such groups in your area, and arrange a meeting with them. Identify ways that your parish can work to support their efforts.

2. Organize or join a social justice committee in your parish. Take part in social concerns organizations in your area, volunteer in a local soup kitchen, or organize a food drive for a local food pantry.

3. Discuss with your group the structures that do not adequately serve those who are poor. Is there sufficient public transportation; are there institutions that can match willing workers with jobs; is there affordable housing; are rental properties and motels maintained and effectively inspected? Pick one such issue and campaign to make positive changes. Support organizations that care for the poor, either by volunteering to help or through financial support.

4. Policies that promote "green jobs" in areas such as energy efficiency and renewable energy can create opportunities for the unemployed and underemployed while also benefitting society. Organize an educational forum about this in your parish and encourage parishioners to contact their elected officials in support of such policies.

5. Write to your lawmakers and elected officials and urge them to act with urgency to put care for creation, the poor, and the common good ahead of short-term special interests. Sign up for alerts from faith-based

How Can I Make a Difference?

When people first become aware of the seriousness and scope of the threat that climate change poses to humanity, they may feel overwhelmed. They may wonder, "What can I, as one person, do to make a difference?" In this book, near the end of each session, there is a section called "Invitation to Act." Each session includes several examples of actions participants or small groups working together can take. These are just examples, and participants should not be limited by them. During your small-group meetings, your faith sharing may lead you to take other actions on behalf of the earth's ecology.

The issues related to climate change and the environment are wide ranging, so you may want to take some time to discern the ways in which you want to take action. Which issues concern you the most? Which issues affect you personally? Which issues affect your state or region? Do you have family and friends overseas or in other parts of the country? Which issues are affecting them? Access to safe sources of water? Rising sea levels? Promoting clean and renewable sources of energy? The effect of hydraulic fracturing (fracking) on local communities? The impact on the poor of rising temperatures and sea levels, or of pollution of air and water?

Each of us has a different set of skills and gifts. What are yours? Planning events to increase awareness? Organizing petition drives? Working with the media? Writing letters to the editors of local news organizations or legislators' offices? Visiting legislators to inform them of the facts and your concerns?

Is there an environmental commission in your town or county? Is there a county-wide or state-wide association of environmental commissions? What kinds of programs do these commissions offer; what kinds of advocacy organizations such as the U.S. Conference of Catholic Bishops, GreenFaith, and the Catholic Climate Covenant.

6. Research how communities of color and low-income communities in the United States suffer from excessive pollution and lack of access to clean air, healthy food, and open space. Determine how your group or your parish can publicize these issues, and work with community leaders to address them.

projects do they undertake? What could you learn from programs sponsored by such a commission? What how might you assist such a commission as a volunteer?

Often, because these issues are new to many people of faith, it's wise to start slowly and modestly, organizing some events to raise awareness in your parish and to see which members of your community are interested. You can then convene a planning meeting of these people to determine some of your longer-term goals.

We also want to share a few thoughts about the importance, and the challenges, related to environmental advocacy. There is great value in individuals taking part in the political process. Legislators know that for each person who makes the effort to call their offices, there are hundreds, possibly thousands, of constituents who feel the same way. If you become an advocate on climate and energy issues—particularly as a voice for the most vulnerable—you will be working against interests with considerable funding and sophistication. Many of those who oppose environmental protection represent lobbies that are politically and economically powerful. But there is strength and power in numbers. Consider joining your efforts at the local level with those of others working on these issues by getting involved with a faith-based ecological advocacy organization such as the Catholic Climate Covenant or GreenFaith.

Learn More

Catholic Climate Covenant, **www.catholicclimatecovenant.org**

GreenFaith, **www.greenfaith.org**

Closing Prayer

Pray together:

Loving and gracious God, we thank you for the gift of your Son, Jesus Christ.
In teaching us of the "blessedness" of the poor in our midst,
he helps us to understand that in your eyes we are worthy,
not because of reputation, title or wealth,
but because of the Spirit that renews and transforms us daily.

Pause for individual members to bring specific cases of poverty and exclusion to prayer.

Help us to be sensitive to the promptings of that Spirit and act on them,
so that in this changing world we may help one another
grow to the fullness of what God has called us to become.
We ask this through Christ, our Lord. Amen.

Looking Ahead

Prepare for the next session by prayerfully reading

— Session 5, "Creation: The First Book of Revelation"

— Psalm 104:24-30

— Pope Francis' encyclical *Laudato Si'*, paragraphs 62-88.

Learn More

U.S. Conference of Catholic Bishops, "Global Climate Change:
A Plea for Dialogue, Prudence, and the Common Good":
**http://www.usccb.org/issues-and-action/human-life-and-dignity/
environment/global-climate-change-a-plea-for-dialogue-prudence-
and-the-common-good.cfm**

For information about green jobs, visit
http://www.greenforall.org/jobs_prosperity.

GreenFaith's environmental justice resource center offers materials
to help faith communities understand the link between pollution and
poverty and to empower them to take action in response:
http://www.greenfaith.org/resource-center/justice

"The Spirit of God has filled the world with possibilities, and therefore, from the very heart of things, something new can emerge. Nature is nothing other than a certain kind of art, namely God's art, impressed upon things, whereby those things are moved to a determinate end."

Pope Francis, Laudato Si', 80

SESSION 5

Creation:
The First Book of Revelation

Focus for This Session

God's creating hand is visible in what he has made.

Suggested Environment

On a small table, which may be decorated with the color of the liturgical season, you may have a Bible, a burning candle, and a crucifix, in addition to articles representative of the environment, such as water, stones, soil, or plant life.

Gather

Opening Prayer

Pray together:

Gracious, loving Creator God,
how awesome, lovely, and manifold are the works of your creation.
In wisdom you have made them all:
from the tiniest ant to the huge whales of the sea,
from the all-seeing hawk to the slow-moving caterpillar.

Yet into this incredible variety you have formed a grammar of creation,
so that each created entity has its own role, its own relationship,
and its own value within the whole.

Help us, Creator God, to recognize the many ways in which you speak to us
in the rhythms of your beautiful world
so that we may come to cherish and respect more deeply
our own relationships with you and the earth that you have created.

Amen.

Song Suggestion

"For the Beauty of the Earth" (OCP)
Digital playlist available at www.renewintl.org/creation

Living Our Faith

Share briefly your experience of putting into effect the action you chose after the last session.

See: Tiny Creature Reflects the Divine

The creative hand of God can be seen at work in something as delicate as the monarch butterfly—a species whose numbers are in decline. It is called the "monarch" because of its regal black body with white spots and bright orange wings and black borders. Female monarchs in North America lay their eggs, the size of pinpoints, on the undersides of milkweed plants, one egg for each plant. The monarch chooses the milkweed because its sticky milk is toxic and poisonous to all predators. The eggs hatch, and small caterpillars emerge. These caterpillars feed on the milkweed before suspending themselves on the underside of a leaf or branch and forming a chrysalis (pupa). After about two weeks, a mature monarch emerges from the chrysalis and becomes an adult, winged butterfly. The entire process is repeated several times before the monarchs, which cannot survive harsh winters, fly several thousand miles to winter roosts in a mountainous region sixty miles west of Mexico City. At their winter sites, they cluster together by the thousands in colonies in a semi-dormant state. Come the end of March, the monarchs make their way back to where they came from in the North. How do these small, fragile, winged creatures manage this migration? The process is part of "God's art, impressed upon things, whereby those things are moved to a determinate end" (*Laudato Si'*, 80). Nature is a constant source of wonder and awe, a continuing revelation of the divine.

The Word of God

Psalm 104:24-30

The Hand of God Sustains Creation

Moment of Silent Reflection

With the monarch butterfly in mind, what word, phrase or image from the scripture reading touched your heart or spoke to your life?

Invitation to Share

1. Share the word, phrase, or image from the scripture reading that touched your heart.

2. What aspect of our created world do you find awe-inspiring, mysterious, and evocative of the divine? Explain.

Reflection

St. Bonaventure, a Franciscan theologian of the sixteenth century, said that creation is the first and primary book of revelation. By this he meant that to "read" the book of creation one didn't have to be a trained theologian or scripture scholar. To appreciate the love and beauty of God manifest in creation, all one has to do is "see" and reflect. Thoughtful observation recognizes the beauty, intricacy, mystery, and harmony of creation. Additional insight yields deeper awareness and meaning: "How varied are your works, O Lord. In wisdom you have wrought them all."

While we appreciate our environment and recognize its beauty, we may also take it for granted. We enjoy its mountains and valleys, seashores and lakes, its parks and nature preserves. We marvel at the graceful deer, the colorful birds, and the delicate butterflies. But we should also be aware that our beautiful earth is under siege, and its natural elements—including the monarch butterfly—are imperiled. We should be aware of both this problem and of our moral duty to address it.

Pope Francis, in his encyclical *Laudato Si'*, tells us that God has written a precious book "whose letters are the multitude of created things present in the universe" (85). Soil, water, mountains—everything is, as it were, an expression of the sacred. "Alongside revelation properly so-called, contained in Scripture," Pope Francis writes, quoting a catechesis of St. John Paul II, "there is a divine manifestation in the blaze of the sun and the fall of night." Such manifestations of creation allow us to discover a teaching or message that God wants to pass on to us. That teaching, essentially, is our awe at God's majesty, creativity, and love and our relationship to all creation. We are taught to recognize our origin, our life's pattern, and our destiny. Everything comes from God, exemplifies God, and returns to God. This calls for self-understanding, courage, and a willingness to take action. Without this self-knowledge, there will be no knowledge of creation as our home and the womb of our birth. We won't understand why we must care for it and protect it. Without embodying the giftedness and sacredness of creation, we will not be able to respond and act when it groans in pain, or when it is manipulated or abused. Who will speak up and do something about polluted beaches, lakes, and rivers? Who will speak up for the poor who lack fresh water? Creation is the writing finger of God. It is telling us something. We who read the book of creation are called upon to respond in a responsible manner.

Only when we can recognize creatures as expressions of God's overflowing love can we recognize the source of our lives as well. The love that gave birth to all creatures is the same love that has brought us into existence. This love of God for all creation, as expressed by the psalmist, also unites us in fond affection with Brother Sun, Sister Moon, Brother River, and Mother Earth. We are all a part of the pilgrimage of creation.

> "A spirituality which forgets God as all-powerful and Creator is not acceptable. That is how we end up worshipping earthly powers, or ourselves usurping the place of God, even to the point of claiming an unlimited right to trample his creation underfoot. The best way to restore men and women to their rightful place, putting an end to their claim of absolute dominion over the earth, is to speak once more of the figure of a Father who creates and who alone owns the world. Otherwise, human beings will always try to impose their own laws and interests on reality."
>
> Pope Francis, *Laudato Si'*, 75

The second book of revelation, Sacred Scripture, speaks to us not only of creation but also of incarnation. It speaks to us of a God who made us and who also desires to share his life with us in and through the person of Jesus Christ. The love which gave birth to all creation was also the love that gave birth to Jesus. That God became human, one like us, is central to the Christian faith. Jesus was born of matter, having a human body like any one of us. The self-communication of God to the world in the person of Jesus Christ as a child of the earth is the key that holds together the whole adventure of Christian faith.

Matter is dignified by the presence of the earthy humanity of Jesus. Matter now becomes the bearer of God's powerful Spirit and the medium of new creation. What happened in and through the witness of Jesus Christ represents a new stage of what we are meant to become as human beings and what is intended for all of creation. Jesus Christ is the paradigm or exemplar of human life and of what we are called to become.

Jesus proclaimed the present reality of "the reign of God" which evoked the possibility, in the here and now, of a new relationship between God and humankind and all created reality. The Gospels are filled with examples drawn from the earthiness of first-century Palestine: grapes, thorn-bushes, figs and thistles, mustard seeds and leaven. To the poor, the sick, the outcasts his message was one of hope and transformation. Jesus' words and deeds gave witness to the merciful compassion of God who cares deeply about giving life and wholeness. Salvation does not take place outside the created world.

God's self-giving love offers further meaning to the Paschal Mystery.

The death of Jesus on the cross was an outstanding expression of self-giving love.

His resurrection was a completion of his self-giving and the celebration of a resurrected life. This pattern of death and new life is similar to the pattern of all creation within the circle of life. All creatures are moving forward to a common point, which is God in that transcendent fullness where the risen Christ embraces and illumines all things. This leads us to direct our gaze to the end of time, when the Son will deliver all things to the Father so that "God may be everything to everyone" (1 Cor 15:28).

Invitation to Share

Take a few moments of silence to reflect on the following questions. Then share your reflections.

1. The author writes that creation "is telling us something" about how it is being neglected or misused. How have you experienced this?

2. How do you respond internally when you learn of a living species that is declining or is actually in danger of extinction?

3. What relationship do you see between Jesus, who lived on the earth in flesh and blood, and the state of the natural world in which you live now?

Invitation to Act

Being together and sharing in a small Christian community fosters growth in our faith and in our spirituality. However, no communal sharing is complete without a serious commitment to putting our faith into practice. In this session we have reflected on creation as the first book of revelation of God's creative presence in the world. How does this inspire us to act? The following are examples.

1. Spend time contemplating the fact that something very familiar—the sun, the moon, the air you breathe, the water you drink—exists, as you do, because of the continuous creative activity of God. Write in your journal about how this contemplation affects your perception of your place in the natural world.

2. As an individual or with your group, contact a nursing home, hospice, group home, or corrections facility in your community and ask how you might help organize and outdoor activity that could help those being cared for to feel more closely connected to the world around them. Act on this suggestion.

3. Take note of the products you buy that are packaged in plastic bags, shrink wrap, or bottles that all are potentially hazardous to human health and to the wellbeing of other creatures that share the planet with us. Take steps to reduce your use of these plastics.

4. What can you do to modernize the inefficient energy producers in your life? Does your home need an energy-efficient furnace, water cooler, air conditioner, or refrigerator?

Closing Prayer

Pray together:

Loving, gracious Creator God,
your Son, Jesus Christ, once told us:
"Peace I leave with you, my peace I give you.
Do not let your hearts be troubled, and do not let them be afraid."

May our sharing this day be a source of blessing and peace for all of us.

Bless our friends and families with your abiding joy and peace.

Bless also those who are called to be peacemakers,
and may we who enjoy the peace and joy from our love
of the created world share that peace with all around us.

We ask this through Christ, the Prince of Peace. Amen.

Looking Ahead

Prepare for the next session by prayerfully reading

— Session 6, "Why Do We Have an Environmental Crisis?"

— Luke 12:16-21

— Pope Francis's encyclical, *Laudato Si'*, paragraphs 89-114.

Learn More

Care for Creation, A Franciscan Spirituality of the Earth, Ilia Delio, Keith Douglass Warner, and Pamela Wood; St. Anthony Messenger Press, 2007.

"We have to accept that technological products are not neutral, for they create a framework which ends up conditioning lifestyles and shaping social possibilities along the lines dictated by the interests of certain powerful groups. Decisions which may seem purely instrumental are in reality decisions about the kind of society we want to build."

Pope Francis, *Laudato Si'*, 107

SESSION 6

Why Do We Have an Environmental Crisis?

Focus for This Session

We endanger ourselves and future generations when we act as if resources are inexhaustible.

Suggested Environment

On a small table, which may be decorated with the color of the liturgical season, you may have a Bible, a burning candle, and a crucifix, in addition to articles representative of the environment, such as water, stones, soil, or plant life.

Gather

Opening Prayer

Pray together:

Gracious, loving Creator God,
we praise you this day for the gift of light
that overcomes the darkness of night.

We bless you for sun, wind, and rain,
and change of seasons that help us to appreciate
the manifold gifts of creation.

As we begin this session, open the gifts
of our minds and hearts
to the promptings of your Spirit
so that our prayer, reflection,
and interaction with one another
may fill us with joy and hope
as we strive to walk in your ways. Amen.

Song Suggestion

"Come, You Thankful People, Come" (OCP)
Digital playlist available at www.renewintl.org/creation

Living Our Faith

Share briefly your experience of putting into effect the action you chose after the last session.

See: A River With No Future?

In the United States, the Colorado River runs through seven states and into Mexico. The water is used by over 36 million people and irrigates close to four million acres of land. The water is used by those millions for their day-to-day needs, and it helps to support around 15 percent of crops grown in the United States. It has also been named the most endangered river in the nation, due to outdated water management, drought, and overuse, according to American Rivers, an organization dedicated to protecting U.S. waterways.

The Colorado delta once covered two million acres near the river's mouth at the Gulf of California. For 1,000 years the Cucapà tribe hunted, fished, and farmed in this very fertile area, where only two inches of rain falls annually. With the construction of dams over the years, the demand for Colorado River water now exceeds the supply. People use the water for drinking, agriculture, and fishing, and now a large part of the river supports a huge recreation industry. Consequently, the economy of the surrounding states, as well as the life needs of the indigenous people who live in the area, are greatly impacted as access to the river shrinks. Obviously, there are off-setting values, each with its promoters. It is up to those whose lives depend on the ecological systems of the Colorado basin to come together and to provide solutions. Otherwise, reliable water supplies and a healthy river will not exist for future generations. As the indigenous say: *No agua, no vida* (No water, no life).

The Word of God

Luke 12:16-21
True Riches are with God

Moment of Silent Reflection

With the Colorado River in mind, what word, phrase, or image from the scripture reading touched your heart or spoke to your life?

Invitation to Share

1. Share the word, phrase, or image from the scripture reading that touched your heart.

2. What point was Jesus making in this parable? What is wrong with storing one's treasures for future use?

Reflection

As in the case of the Colorado River, the environmental crisis is rooted in the rapid rate of change taking place in our times. Over the past two hundred years, we have moved from the horse and buggy to suburban utility vehicles, from the "Flying Jenny" to a transcontinental airline industry. Major advances in the areas of medicine, communication systems, information technology, and digital engineering have improved the quality of our lives. We are living longer. We have more creature comforts. Who can deny the progress? "Never has humanity had such power over itself, yet nothing ensures that it will be used wisely, particularly when we consider how it is currently being used" (*Laudato Si'*, 104).

Consider the great wars and the international tensions of the past century, the use of atomic bombs, and the threat of even more powerful hydrogen bombs. Consider the environmental conflicts and acts of aggression taking place around the globe and the threats of terrorism in our own country. The power of modern technology is prodigious. It all depends who is using the power, and how. Unfortunately, an increase in power does not always mean an increase in progress, security, fraternity, and respect among people. There will always be the need for sound ethical principles and the spiritual grounding capable of inspiring clear-minded self-restraint. Enormous technological development has not always been accompanied by human responsibility, sound values, and right conscience. This reality has substantial environmental implications. While some technologies have a beneficial environmental impact, this is not always the case, and some technologies have genuinely negative environmental impacts even if they do create other benefits, as evidenced by the enormous levels of toxic electronic waste from millions of computers, cell phones, and tablets which represent a growing health threat in the poor countries and neighborhoods where this waste is discarded. When it comes to the environment, technology is not neutral.

The problem goes even deeper. It also involves the manner in which we regard and use our natural resources. People have always intervened in nature. It appears, however, that the relationship between human beings and material objects has become confrontational. Many people think and act as if there were an infinite quantity of natural resources such as water and petroleum. Many of us behave as if non-renewable resources are easy to find,

---

Here are some of the regrettable consequences of humans acting as if they were God.

- **Failing to recognize the intrinsic value of a person who is poor, an embryo, a person with disabilities.**

- **Failing to value other human beings in general.**

- **Failing to appreciate the importance of interpersonal relationships.**

- **Failure to appreciate creation's inherent goodness and dignity.**

- **Treating others as "mere objects" to be sold, exploited or abused.**

- **Instead of being cooperators with God in the work of creation, acting as if one were God and acting in ways that are contrary to the rhythms of nature and destructive of creation.**

- **Losing a sense of responsibility for the world by failing to use one's human gifts of knowledge, will, freedom, and responsibility unless it serves one's own selfish purposes.**

- **Giving absolute priority to immediate convenience. Everything is irrelevant unless it serves one's own interests.**

- **Using and consuming more than one needs.**

- **Failing to recognize that all of life is inter-connected and inter-dependent, and it does not belong exclusively to any self-appointed "master of the universe."**

---

and that negative effects of exploiting our natural resources can be easily absorbed. Nature itself, which denies that its resources are inexhaustible, is not brought into the conversation. To the extent that such a model shapes the way we behave as nation-states, industries, and individual men and women, the environment suffers.

Technological products—including smart phones, plasma TVs, self-parking cars, and commonplace items such as plastic water bottles and coffee "pods"—are not neutral. Promoted by powerful financial and commercial forces, the availability of these and other products creates a framework, a way of thinking, which encourages us to strive for certain lifestyles. These forces can shape consumer attitudes toward purchasing goods and services: the kinds of clothing we must have to be fashionable, the smart phones we use, the cars we drive, the food we eat, and even, sad to say, the type of society we are building. Deluding ourselves into thinking that we have limitless resources also leads to wasteful and hyped-up consumerism. It's so easy to buy more, far more, than we need, because there is so much of it available—and with discounts! But Mother Earth is telling us that our resources are limited. We need the moral principles and the wisdom to show us ways of restraint and the values of a simple lifestyle.

> **"Men and women have constantly intervened in nature, but for a long time this meant being in tune with and respecting the possibilities offered by the things themselves. It was a matter of receiving what nature itself allowed, as if from its own hand. Now, by contrast, we are the ones to lay our hands on things, attempting to extract everything possible from them while frequently ignoring or forgetting the reality in front of us. Human beings and material objects no longer extend a friendly hand to one another; the relationship has become confrontational."**
>
> Pope Francis, *Laudato Si'*, 106

It becomes difficult to counteract the dominant models of technology. They are very attractive and powerful. They can diminish and weaken the capacities for alternate choices of lifestyle. The economy, on the other hand, looks at technology with a view toward how to maximize profits. There is nothing wrong with making a profit. But the problem is in determining how much profit is acceptable, and what is also owed to the common good and to those who are living at a subsistence level. For people whose values respect both the limitations of natural resources and the right of all people to acquire the necessities of life, this becomes an important discussion that can and should lead to alternate ethical horizons. Nobody is suggesting a return to the Stone Age. However, as Pope Francis writes in his encyclical, "we do need to slow down and look at reality in a different way, to appropriate the positive and sustainable progress which has been made, but also to recover the values and the great goals swept away by our unrestrained delusions of grandeur" (*Laudato Si'*, 114).

When humans, inspired by such delusions, regard themselves as the center of the universe, then nature is regarded as a cold body of facts, a mere object of utility, as raw material to be hammered into useful shapes. The intrinsic dignity of the world is thus compromised. When human beings fail to find their true place and role in this world, they misunderstand themselves and end up acting against themselves. There is only one God, and it is not we! When Adam ate of the forbidden fruit in the Garden of Eden (Gn. 2:16ff.) he acted as if he were God. He went against his nature, and painful consequences followed. Acting as if we were the center of the universe (anthropocentrism) gives rise to an erroneous understanding of the relationship between human beings and the world. It leads to what is known in psychoanalysis as "the false self," in this case the false impression that we are masters of the world rather than faithful stewards as we are called to be. That illusion has led to many of the problems that already plague the environment and threaten its future.

Once we start acting like God, everything starts falling apart. Morally speaking that is referred to as sin. In effect, we can become like the rich man spoken of in today's scriptural reading. He had wealth, and with that some power, but that did not indicate any increase in wisdom.

Invitation to Share

Take a few moments of silence to reflect on the following questions. Then share your reflections.

1. What are the greatest technological changes that you have experienced in your own lifetime? In what ways have these changes improved the quality of life? In what ways have they diminished it? Have there been unintended environmental consequences of these technological developments?

2. How do you strike a balance between having what you need in order to live safely and comfortably and sharing your resources with those whose lives are at best marginal?

3. How do you understand the term "wasteful consumerism"? Can you give an example(s) from society? From your own life?

Invitation to Act

Being together and sharing in a small Christian community fosters growth in our faith and in our spirituality. However, no communal sharing is complete without a serious commitment to putting our faith into practice. In this session we have reflected on why we now have an ecological crisis. How does this inspire us to act? The following are examples.

1. Research the industries, institutions, organizations, or groups in your area that are most sensitive to environmental issues. What is it that indicates such sensitivity? Write a letter of congratulations for such responsible behavior.

2. Search your house for obsolete electronic and electrical devices, cables, and power cords. Research how these objects can be recycled or safely disposed of, and act on what you learn.

3. Choose a particular type of technology and take a break from its use while thinking about how feasible it would be to make this change permanently. For example, take public transportation instead of driving to work in your own car. Turn off the air conditioning in your home for 24 hours. Turn off all lights when rooms are not in use. Turn on the television only when someone is watching it. Pick up your mobile phone only when you really need it, and turn it off when you're driving or when you're sharing a meal with your family or friends.

4. To combat consumerism, avoid compulsive purchases. Wait a week to see if you still want or need an item.

5. Find ways to reduce your trash generation such as composting food scraps and purchasing milk in reusable bottles.

6. Consider the footprint of products before you buy them: from resource extraction to production, distribution, consumption, and disposal. Who is making this product? How and where is this made? Using what resources? How long will it last? When you do make purchases, choose items with compostable or biodegradable packaging.

Closing Prayer

Pray together:

Good and gracious God, we stand in awe of your power
in creating this great planet, our common home,
which we cherish and enjoy.

Help us to see it anew for the wonder that it is.

Open our eyes, enlighten our minds, and show us the ways
by which we can preserve it and respect its laws and rhythms.

Teach us to be wise, faithful and responsible caretakers of its gifts
that we only borrow for our lifetime.

May we receive them from you with glory and praise
and pass them down with gratitude to those who follow us. Amen.

Looking Ahead

Prepare for the next session by prayerfully reading

— Session 7, "Responsible Use of Technology"

— Wisdom 6:2-8

— Pope Francis's encyclical, *Laudato Si'*, paragraphs 115-136.

"A technology severed from ethics will not easily be able to limit its own power."

Pope Francis, Laudato Si', 136

SESSION 7

Responsible Use of Technology

Focus for This Session

Technological progress must serve the needs of all.

Suggested Environment

On a small table, which may be decorated with the color of the liturgical season, you may have a Bible, a burning candle, and a crucifix, in addition to articles representative of the environment, such as water, stones, soil, or plant life.

Gather

Opening Prayer

Divide the group in two and pray the following:

Group 1:	Gracious, loving Creator God, from the beginning of time and space, your power and wisdom have shown forth.
Group 2:	We recognize signs of your caring presence in the brilliance of galaxies, stars, and sun.
Group 1:	We marvel at the precision of their movements and interaction.
Group 2:	They tell us that you are mystery, present in our midst, yet utterly beyond.

Group 1:   We are blessed to know you more
through the powerful presence
of your Son and our Lord, Jesus Christ.

Group 2:   For those times when we have acted as if you did not exist,
for those times when we acted as if we were gods, forgive us.

All: **May our sharing help us better
to appreciate our true relationship**   .
with you and with all that you have created. Amen.

Song Suggestion

"Thanks Be to God" (OCP)
Digital playlist available at www.renewintl.org/creation

Living Our Faith

Share briefly your experience of putting into effect the action you chose after the last session.

See: Progress at Any Cost?

In February 2015, thousands of people braved the harsh cold of Washington, D.C., to rally in opposition to construction of the Keystone XL pipeline. This project, begun in 2010, would have involved transporting raw, highly polluting tar-sands oil 1,179 miles through the American heartland, from Alberta, Canada to refineries on the Gulf Coast. At capacity, the pipeline would have been capable of delivering 830,000 barrels of crude oil per day. Three phases of the project are in operation, and the fourth was awaiting U.S. government approval. This final phase could have affected some of the most environmentally sensitive areas of the country. Environmentalists point out that the pipeline would endanger indigenous communities that lie in its path and imperil the immense Ogallala aquifer, a major source of irrigation and drinking water for the people of the Great Plains. It could also result in many people being exposed to a high level of toxins emitted from tar-sands oil refining. Most important, argue opponents, is that completing the pipeline would have been a step into the past instead of a shift toward a clean-energy future. Why continue our dependence on energy derived from fossil fuels, they asked, when we should be investing in safe renewable sources of energy instead?

On the other hand, major oil businesses, a slight majority of the U.S. Congress and good portion of the American populace supported the Keystone XL project, arguing that the pipeline would have been one of the safest and most advanced in North America and would have provided more jobs, additional energy, security, and economic benefits for the United States. But those arguments were outweighed by an intense campaign by groups and individuals concerned about further degradation of the environment. After the U.S. government received a record number of comments opposing the pipeline, President Obama used his authority to reject the project in November 2015.

The Word of God

Wisdom 6:2-8
The Mighty Will Be Judged Mightily

Moment of Silent Reflection

With the Keystone Pipeline, or similar projects, in mind, what word, phrase, or image from the scripture reading touched your heart or spoke to your life?

Invitation to Share

1. Share the word, phrase, or image from the scripture reading that touched your heart.

2. The writer of the Book of Wisdom upbraids those who do not use their wisdom and power wisely. Do you feel called to influence authority figures who do not exhibit any care or concern for a healthy environment? Why or why not? How would you do that?

Reflection

"Integral ecology" is a term that Pope Francis uses often in his encyclical to describe a moral imperative, connecting protection of creation, sustainable development, and care for the poor. The moral imperative certainly applies to the responsible use of modern technology. The principle of integral ecology may provide useful guidelines for shedding more light on controversies pertaining to the relative values or disadvantages of projects such as the Keystone XL pipeline.

Pope Francis has written this encyclical not just for Christians but for all people of good faith and conscience. He is not writing as a scientist, politician, or economist but as a global moral leader. He appeals to all of us "for a new dialogue about how we are shaping the future of our planet." The pope uses the term "dialogue" very often in the encyclical. He does not pretend to have all of the answers for solving environmental problems. He has reached out to influential scientists, business people, public officials, theologians, and philosophers to give substance and authority to his arguments. For a broader geographical and cultural perspective, he also consulted with representatives of the more affluent Northern Hemisphere as well as those from the poorer countries of the Southern Hemisphere. One need only consult the 173 footnotes of the pope's encyclical to appreciate the all-embracing vision of the document.

The reason for highlighting here the religious and moral role of Pope Francis in this matter is found in two important words in the title of this session: "responsible use." Responsible use of technology will not take place without the application of ethical principles. Technology, economics, and politics are important and powerful forces. But unless those forces are counter-balanced by a moral and social vision, little will be accomplished to heal and restore a fragile world. Today's reading from the Book of Wisdom is a reminder for those in power to seek the ways of wisdom in their service to others. Wisdom is seen as an expression of God's presence. The one who is truly wise is seen as doing God's will in the world. However, some rulers and "those who have power over the multitude and lord it over throngs of people" can be enticed by complete freedom of thought and expression to hold themselves arrogantly independent of God, acting in ways that contribute to the misery of the powerless. As verse eight of the scriptural reading suggests, "for those in power a rigorous scrutiny impends."

> "Work is a necessity, part of the meaning of life on this earth, a path to growth, human development, and personal fulfilment. Helping the poor financially must always be a provisional solution in the face of pressing needs. The broader objective should always be to allow them a dignified life through work. Yet the orientation of the economy has favored a kind of technological progress in which the costs of production are reduced by laying off workers and replacing them with machines. This is yet another way in which we can end up working against ourselves."
>
> Pope Francis, *Laudato Si'*, 128

Advances in technology over the past two hundred years have provided many benefits to humankind. Progress in the areas of nuclear energy, biotechnology, information technology, and knowledge of our DNA has been enormous. Thank God for human creativity and genius! But modern technology has also given rise to power never seen before. Technology has unleashed an unprecedented capacity to kill and maim, as we remember from Hiroshima and Nagasaki. Increase in power is not necessarily progress for life on this planet. For all of the major benefits

Investing for an Integral Ecology

People of faith as well as faith-based communities have an opportunity to have an impact as they make decisions about the investment of their assets. They can view their investments solely as means of funding financial objectives and missions, or they can view investment decisions themselves as expressions of their moral values and instruments of mission. Individual and institutional investors alike can use the power of their investments to influence the managers and other stakeholders to implement socially and environmentally responsible corporate practices. They can hold corporations accountable to shareholders and the public for the effects of their policies and actions.

Some typical issues around which investors engage corporations include abortifacients, access to health care, access to water, antipersonnel landmines, board of directors diversity, climate change, contraception, embryonic stem cell research/human cloning, environmental justice, executive compensation, gender discrimination, genetically modified foods, global codes of conduct, human rights, human trafficking, Native American land rights, predatory lending, pharmaceutical pricing, pornography, production and sale of weapons, racial justice, tobacco sales, toxic chemicals, and violence in video games.

With respect to climate change, there is a growing movement to consider if and how investors should act against fossil fuel companies. Whether you directly own shares in companies or you own shares in bonds or mutual funds, you have several options. You can buy shares of companies, bonds, or funds whose climate-change policies and actions you approve of. You can sell shares of companies, bonds, or funds whose climate-change actions and policies you disapprove of. You can use your voice and vote as a shareholder.

If you own shares in fossil fuel companies, you may choose to divest if you believe that shareholder activism is not sufficient to change these companies' long-term business plans to extract and burn dangerous levels of fossil fuels. To ensure that a company knows why you have divested, you should inform the company's investor relations department. Additionally, should you choose to divest, it is critical to "reinvest" in companies and financial products that help build a clean energy economy.

Let your local, state, and federal officials know that you want them to take action against climate change and support the path to a low-carbon energy economy. You can join thousands of other investors, large and small, who have petitioned the Securities and Exchange Commission to require companies to disclose their political contribution and lobbying expenditures. Because numerous prominent companies pay dues to, make contributions to, or sit on the boards of organizations that oppose legislation and regulation to curb greenhouse gas emissions, by pushing companies to disclose their political contributions and lobbying expenditures, investors concerned about climate change can make a difference. US Social Investment Forum (SIF), an association of investment firms and financial professionals, and many institutional investors and investment firms have signed a letter in support of this petition, which you can find on the SEC website (http://www.sec.gov/comments/4-637/4637-11.pdf). You can also add your voice in support of this petition. Public Citizen provides a model letter that you may use or adapt (http://action.citizen.org/p/dia/action/public/?action_KEY=9213).

You can tell your elected representatives that you support regulations to curb greenhouse gas emissions from new and existing power plants. You can also tell your representatives in Congress that you support changes in federal policies that will allow investment in renewable energy developments to receive the same benefits now available to oil, gas, and real estate projects.

You can let your state legislators know that you approve the continuation or expansion of requirements for utilities serving the state to get a certain minimum percentage of their power supply from renewable sources. You can view a state-by-state list of these renewable portfolio standards and related policies at the "DSIRE" Database of State Incentives for Renewables and Efficiency (http://www.dsireusa.org/).

Learn More

Socially Responsible Investment Guidelines, United States Conference of Catholic Bishops, Nov. 12, 2013: **http://www.usccb.org/about/financial-reporting/socially-responsible-investment-guidelines.cfm**

Invested in Change: Faith-Consistent Investing in a Climate-Challenged World, Interfaith Center on Corporate Responsibility, **https://iccr.atavist.com/invested-in-change1m328**

Investing to Curb Climate Change: A Guide for the Institutional Investor, **http://www.ussif.org/files/publications/institutional_climate.pdf**

modern technology has provided, it has also yielded greed, a materialistic and wasteful lifestyle, pollution of the environment, irresponsible use of natural resources, and a tendency to attribute value to people mainly on the basis their wealth or power.

The pope reminds us that "technological products are not neutral, for they create a framework which ends up conditioning lifestyles and shaping social possibilities along the lines dictated by the interests of certain powerful groups" (*Laudato Si'*, 107). The poor are easily forgotten. Modern technology is double-edged; it can have positive and negative values. A moral vision will prompt us to look at ways of applying progress based first on what will serve the common good.

This moral vision is captured in the expression "integral ecology," a more comprehensive way of rethinking and experiencing our relationship with nature. Based on the premise that all creation has come from a common sacred source, everything—living and non-living—is seen as bound together. We are linked together and called to live in right relationship with one another and with all of creation. For one who lives by the principles of integral ecology, there is the conviction that each living being, each bit of created matter, is recognized and valued as expressing the infinite love of God. The earth and everything in it is permeated by the presence and power of the Creator. The earth is not simply empty matter; it is sacred ground.

"Ecology," as a study of all living beings (plants and animals) in relation to our environment, further emphasizes the aspect of connectedness. "Integral ecology" goes beyond the language of mathematics, biology, or better ways of keeping the planet green. It takes us to the heart of what it means to be human. Integral ecology is not some theoretical concept. It speaks of ways in which we relate to one another socially, culturally, and economically. It's the way we are bound together on the earth, our common home. The "integral" dimension of relating to one another must include issues such as the common good, the responsibilities we have to future generations, respecting the poor, caring for our fragile planet, observing a simple lifestyle, living with the awareness that our resources are limited and that sustainable development is therefore essential. The "integral" dimension of ecology connects care for creation, sustainable development, and concern for the poor. Integral ecology rejects current economic patterns and envisions an economic sphere that serves the legitimate needs of individuals and societies rather than exploiting them. It sees that building a pipeline is not simply a matter of moving a mineral from point A to point B in order to produce a product for sale, but a process that has the potential to impact in negative ways human beings, other living things, the earth, and the atmosphere. It demands that economy respect the finite limits of the natural world.

Ultimately, living by the moral tenets of an "integral ecology" calls for faith that is all about relationships. When all is said and done, what really matters is not our stock holdings, the quality or size of our properties, or the material possessions we have amassed. No one has ever seen a U-Haul truck as part of a funeral procession. What matters is the quality of our relationships with our spouses, our families, and those whose lives intersect our own. When "things" rather than relationships with people become the major obsessions of our lives, then we will have failed to love. Life will have diminished. We will have existed, but not really lived.

Certainly, material things will always be needed to sustain us in life. We need material realities to help us attain our goals and values in life with joy and peace and in harmony with all of creation. How we use those material things depends on values and principles that are so much a part of this encyclical. The matter of using technology in a responsible manner will mean becoming immersed—body, mind and spirit—in the life-giving orientation of integral ecology. Pope Francis has given us the principles, the challenge, and the encouragement. We are the ones who must put this into practice in our homes, our schools, our churches, our places of work and leisure. We have only one common home in which we are bound together. Our deepest desire is to abide together in mutual respect, fraternity, peace, and love.

Invitation to Share

Take a few moments of silence to reflect on the following questions. Then share your reflections.

1. Pope Francis reminds us that technological products are not neutral; rather, they influence lifestyles and shape social possibilities. How has technology shaped your lifestyle and your social possibilities?

2. Do you resist or enthusiastically embrace new technology (such as mobile phones and e-readers)? Why do you think you respond as you do?

3. "Integral ecology" suggests that everyone and everything in the world we inhabit is connected in a vital way. How do you feel your way of life affects the world beyond your immediate surroundings? Are you satisfied with your impact? Why? Would you like to change it? How?

Invitation to Act

Being together and sharing in a small Christian community fosters growth in our faith and in our spirituality. However, no communal sharing is complete without a serious commitment to putting our faith into practice. In this session we have reflected on the responsible use of technology. How does this inspire us to act? The following are examples.

1. Continue to consider and adopt ways of saving energy. For example:

   — Instead of using your car, walk when possible. Adjust your thermostat and the temperature in your water heater so as not to use any more energy than absolutely necessary.

   — The next time you stop briefly at a convenience store, do not leave your car engine idling.

   — Use reusable bags when shopping at the supermarket.

   — Use the most energy-efficient appliances you can afford.

   — Run dishwashers and washing machines with full loads only.

   — Turn off energy strips and surge protectors, when not in use for long periods of time.

   — Use energy-saving light-emitting diode (LED) or compact fluorescent (CFL) bulbs in your home or place of business.

2. Instead of checking your email or social media accounts on your smart phone the next time you are waiting online, engage in conversation with other people.

3. Ask your family and friends to turn off their mobile phones when they are visiting you or joining you in an outing. Voluntarily adopt the same practice yourself, and make a point of telling those who will benefit from having your whole attention.

4. Power off your mobile phone—handheld or not—whenever you are driving.

5. Are you and your family open to considering ways that you might simplify your lives—for the purpose of your own spiritual growth and the protection of God's creation? You can commit to using less fossil fuel, eating less meat, reducing the number of toxic chemicals you use, or other action steps.

Closing Prayer

Pray together:

Loving and gracious God,
we thank you for the gift of wise and responsible people in our lives.

Through the power of your Spirit they are for us
ways of truth and powerful examples of your guiding presence.

We pray in a special way for the prophets in our midst,
who prick our consciences and challenge us to view life in a different way.

We thank you in a special way for our good and wise shepherd, Pope Francis,
who helps us to view our created world with eyes of love.

Pause to allow members to ask God's help in healing specific problems in the environment.

We ask all this through Christ, our Lord. Amen.

Looking Ahead

Prepare for the next session by prayerfully reading

— Session 8, "Integral Ecology Leads to a Healthy Living Environment"

— 1 Corinthians 12:4-7, 11

— Pope Francis's encyclical, *Laudato Si'*, paragraphs 137-155.

Learn More

The Green Bible, Harper One, Harper Collins, 2008.

National Religious Partnership for the Environment,
www.nrpe.org

"If everything is related, then the health of a society's institutions has consequences for the environment and the quality of human life."

Pope Francis, Laudato Si', 142

SESSION 8

Integral Ecology Leads to a Healthy Living Environment

Focus for This Session

The gifts and the needs of each person are vital.

Suggested Environment

On a small table, which may be decorated with the color of the liturgical season, you may have a Bible, a burning candle, and a crucifix, in addition to articles representative of the environment, such as water, stones, soil, or plant life.

Gather

Opening Prayer

Pray together:

Holy Spirit, by your light
you guide this world towards the Father's love
and accompany creation as it groans in travail.

You also dwell in our hearts and minds
and you inspire us to do what is good.

Praise be to you, now and forever. Amen.

Song Suggestion

"One Bread, One Body" (OCP)
Digital playlist available at www.renewintl.org/creation

Living Our Faith

Share briefly your experience of putting into effect the action you chose after the last session.

See: Religious Orders Unite for the Planet

Jubilee Farm is a 111-acre center for ecology and spirituality sponsored by the Dominican Sisters of nearby Springfield, Illinois. The farm offers retreats, classes on the interdependence of the created world, spiritual direction, and programs for children. Vegetable gardens and an orchard produce chemical-free foods, and the farm conducts classes on maintaining a holistic and sustainable diet. Like everything else on the planet, Jubilee Farm is affected by climate change. Sister Sharon Zayac, OP, director of the facility, noted on the farm's website that Central Illinois has been drifting toward drought for several years, a condition that disrupts the cycle of planting and germination of seeds and hinders the growth of crops. "I'm not sure why we were so stunned a few summers back," she wrote, "when for the first time the well we use to water the garden went dry in midsummer."

Concern for such issues is nothing new to women and men in religious life in the United States. In fact, the Leadership Conference of Women Religious, which represents more than 80 percent of women religious in the United States, including the Dominicans, has been engaged in the ecology movement since its beginnings in the twentieth century. The conference has been a leading voice in raising awareness of problems such as acidification of the oceans, insufficient access to clean water, and the connection between climate change and global hunger. In 2008 the conference and its male counterpart, the Conference of Major Superiors of Men—representing orders of priests, brothers, and seminarians—joined in a resolution "to bring our own experience and charisms to the current conversation on climate change and into action for justice; to seek concrete ways to curb environmental degradation, mitigate its impact on the poorest and most vulnerable people, and restore right relationships among all God's creation; and to foster a consciousness of care for God's creation among all our members, colleagues, institutions and those whom we serve." Pope Francis can hardly have more enthusiastic allies in his call for a dialogue on integral ecology.

The Word of God

1 Corinthians 12:4-7, 11
Many Gifts but One Spirit

Moment of Silent Reflection

In light of the resolutions of the Leadership Conference of Women Religious and the Conference for Major Superiors of Men, what word, phrase, or image from the scripture reading touched your heart or spoke to your life?

Invitation to Share

1. Share the word, phrase, or image from the scripture reading that touched your heart.

2. How would you apply the meaning of this scriptural passage to your parish, or to your small group/faith-sharing community?

Reflection

In the scriptural passage, St. Paul challenges the Christians in Corinth to use their diverse gifts of the Spirit to strengthen the faith life of the community and to create a better quality of human life. As though responding to Paul, women and men in religious life in the United States have committed themselves to use their talents and charisms to contribute to building a more sustainable environment. The common denominator is the role of the Spirit in helping us recognize our place in a world much larger than us and then learn how to actually live in right relationship with one another and all of creation.

Woven into the texture of Pope Francis' encyclical is a similar premise: We are relational beings, living within a natural environment whose components also are interrelated—with each other and with us. This idea that everything is "connected"—the tiniest insect, the tallest giraffe, billions of human beings, and the earth that is our common home—is not just a beautiful concept. This connectedness is, and should be, a part of our consciousness. Whoever we are, whatever we are, whatever our gifts, we are connected in a relationship grounded by our having sprung forth from the very life of God.

If all is connected, then a harmonious relationship should exist between our environment and our social structures: our homes, families, neighborhoods, and the religious, cultural, and social groups that make up our lives. The challenges facing our natural environment and our social structures are not two separate crises—one that is environmental and the other social. There is only one complex crisis with two interrelated components. For example, a large strip mall is being planned for our local area. An integral part of the development process should include bringing together people representing different fields of knowledge, including planning boards and builders, as well as voices representing the local community and scientists who understand the impact of the proposed construction on the natural environment. In that way, planning for the new project would result in a more integral and integrating vision. Whatever tensions exist in the community regarding this new project could be addressed equitably and properly.

Ecosystems are the combination of larger related units: plants, animals, minerals, and people in any given area of the earth. A tiny patch of forest, an oceanfront community, the Mississippi river system, parks, forests, even our back yards, are all ecosystems. Major ecosystems on which life on the earth most heavily depends are those involved in the farming industry, forestry, freshwater and river systems, grasslands, coastlands, and urban centers.

It may seem incongruous to apply the term to cities, but they are perhaps the most familiar of all ecosystems. As fragmented as the different components of cities may appear, they work together as a single organism. Cities aren't just centers of commerce, industry, education, and culture. They are also living entities with green spaces and waterways that bring together nature and the human habitat. Urban areas are experiencing unparalleled expansion as most of the world's population growth is funneled into cities, where half of all people already live. Rapid change is impacting the makeup of cities and is placing major stress on the trees, parks, waterways, transportation, and other life-giving urban amenities. This trend gives rise to Pope Francis' concerns about the importance of using integrated ecological approaches to serve the changing needs of city people.

> **"Authentic development includes efforts to bring about an integral improvement in the quality of human life, and this entails considering the setting in which people live their lives. These settings influence the way we think, feel, and act. In our rooms, our homes, our workplaces and neighborhoods, we use our environment as a way of expressing our identity."**
>
> Pope Francis, *Laudato Si'*, 147

Urban ecosystems provide a range of valuable services without which human society cannot function. For example, they make life livable by dispersing carbon dioxide, providing clean air, purifying water, controlling illnesses, forming soil, and managing waste. In a park, the leaf surfaces of trees can filter out as much as 85 percent of the ambient air pollution with street trees serving as air purifiers providing cleaner air that reduces asthma rates and prevents other respiratory diseases. Urban parks provide space for recreational opportunities and even for aesthetic and spiritual values. For city folks, parks are often the only green and relatively quiet areas where they can slow down and "take a breather." Study after study has shown that without these urban green spaces, people's health declines, crime rises, and the human community becomes frayed. Vacant lots can even be transformed into community gardens providing fresh vegetables, safe places to gather, and beautiful oases in the midst of crowded cities.

Industrial or economic pressures can weaken the social institutions of the human family and dramatically disrupt ecosystems, including the human ecosystem. For example, in some older cities advanced technology has forced factories to close or to move to other parts of the country. The work force is let go. Some may be invited to move with the company to the new location. Due to the loss of employment in the changing area, people move away. Local stores and businesses face financial losses; the neighborhood deteriorates. The quality of life begins to change. Prior industrial pollution is left behind, and new waste-related industries

The St. Francis Pledge

The St. Francis Pledge was introduced by the Catholic Climate Covenant in 2009. Since then thousands of individuals and organizations taken the pledge which simply commits them "to pray, act, and advocate to solve climate change."

How individuals or groups honor the pledge is up to them, but the Catholic Climate Covenant offers suggestions, including setting aside time to pray, as a family or as a church group, for climate action; publishing prayers via a blog or newsletter; investigating solar energy and other renewable options; learning how climate change affects the most vulnerable populations; calculating the "carbon footprint" of one's own home or business and taking steps to reduce it; exploring policies in the workplace that will contribute to protecting and restoring the environment; and connecting with policy-makers, including those in local government in one's own community.

Source: Catholic Climate Covenant, www.catholicclimatecovenant.org

move in because they are unwelcome elsewhere and the community lacks the power to protect itself from this environmental assault.

What takes place in one area can have a direct or indirect influence in other areas. When a city, or a portion of it, diminishes, disrespect for the law becomes more common; crime and violence often follow. For example, drug use in affluent societies at times creates a growing demand for narcotics from poorer urban areas, where people who are desperate for money are drawn into the drug trade.

Integral ecology also involves protecting the historic, artistic, and cultural treasures of humanity in the broadest sense. Culture is more than what is inherited from the past. It also envisions a living, dynamic, participatory present. The forces of economic development tend to diminish the precious heritage of cultures. Progress is not always sensitive to cultural values. Merely technical solutions run the risk of being superficial and of destroying the rich fabric of local cultures. Respecting the rights of peoples and their cultures and the active involvement of local people from within their proper culture, is a basic premise of integral ecology. Quality of life cannot be imposed from without, but must be understood within the world of symbols, rituals, and customs proper to each human group, especially indigenous people. The disappearance of a culture can be just as serious as, or even more serious than, the disappearance of a species of plant or animal. The virtual obliteration of Jewish culture in Eastern Europe during World War II is a notorious instance. And the displacement of people from their cultural and religious homes because of war, famine, or major civil disorders continues to take place in our own time—in Syria and Iraq, for example. If a living context becomes disorderly, chaotic, and noisy, it will impact the quality of people's lives. People deserve a sense of well-being, inner peace, joy—and a good night's sleep! But we also know that impoverished neighborhoods and densely populated settings are often brightened by warm and caring relationships, and wholesome experiences of social life. Pope Francis writes poignantly of such contexts: "I wish to insist that love always proves more powerful. Many people in these conditions are able to weave bonds of belonging and togetherness which convert overcrowding into an experience of community in which the walls of the ego are torn down and the barriers of selfishness overcome" (*Laudato Si'*, 149).

Given the interrelationship between living space and human behavior, it is important for urban planners to take into consideration the views of the people, especially in helping them find housing that will enhance the quality of their lives. To live in one's own home has much to do with personal dignity and possibilities of future growth. The pope urges that construction which affects the urban or rural landscape should take into account how various elements combine to form a whole. He shows a special sensitivity for the poor who cannot afford homes or those who may be living in crowded tenements or unsanitary slums. In all instances, he calls for respect and fairness to all: that opportunities for decent housing be made available to everyone, that conditions for obtaining housing be explained, and that local people be a part of the process in which development is planned and approved. The quality of life in urban areas will also have much to do with systems of transport, traffic, congestion, and levels of pollution from vehicles and power generation. All of these issues are a part of the ecology of life, intended to create for all people the appropriate conditions for a life setting that they can happily call "my home."

Invitation to Share

Take a few moments of silence to reflect on the following questions. Then share your reflections.

1. What aspects of your community—people, landscapes, structures, events—are important to you in your perception of this place as "home"?

2. How does the concept of an ecosystem change or deepen your perception of the town or city you live in?

3. Explain how certain cultural experiences are being diminished or lost because of "progress" in your community.

Invitation to Act

Being together and sharing in a small Christian community fosters growth in our faith and in our spirituality. However, no communal sharing is complete without a serious commitment to putting our faith into practice. In this session we have reflected on how the state of the environment impacts the quality of life for human beings. How does this inspire us to act? The following are examples.

1. Attend your community's planning board meetings to find out what environmental factors are considered with respect to proposed development. As you get familiar with the process, ask questions, give your opinions, and inform your neighbors of what you have learned.

2. Discuss with your neighbors what conditions have a negative effect on the ecosystem in which you all live: speeding traffic, aircraft noise, odors, litter, unkempt public spaces. Find a consensus on the most important of these conditions and plan a course of action to address it.

3. Research opportunities in your area in which you and your neighbors can collectively purchase clean energy (such as energy generated from wind mills).

4. Support your local farming community by joining a CSA. Community-supported agriculture is a way for consumers to buy local, seasonal produce directly from a farmer in their community. A farmer offers a certain number of "shares" to the public. Customers purchase a share (or subscription or membership) at the beginning of the season, and each week they receive a box or bag of fresh produce.

5. Take the St. Francis Pledge: http://www.catholicclimatecovenant.org/pledge

Closing Prayer

Pray together:

Loving, gracious Creator God,
you have blessed us so generously
with the beauty and variety of creation.

You have adorned the world
with so many elegant species of life,
and especially in the form of humankind,
whom you have given to us in an exemplary fashion
in the person of Jesus Christ.

Pause to allow individual members to express thanks for particular aspects of creation that enrich their lives.

We thank you and praise you for our sisters and brothers
with whom we share life and relationships here on earth,
our common home. Amen.

Looking Ahead

Prepare for the next session by prayerfully reading

— Session 9, "The Common Good and Our Common Home"

— Acts 4:32-35

— Pope Francis's encyclical, *Laudato Si'*, paragraphs 156-201.

Learn More

Global Sisters Report, **http://www.globalsistersreport.org**

GreenFaith's GreenWorship resource offers an array of prayers and resources to help integrate environmental care into your parish liturgies: **http://www.greenfaith.org/resource-center/spirit/ greenworship-resource/christian-resource-1/christian-resource**

"The principle of the common good immediately becomes, logically and inevitably, a summons to solidarity and a preferential option for the poorest of our brothers and sisters... The notion of the common good also extends to future generations."

Pope Francis, *Laudato Si'*, 158, 159

SESSION 9

The Common Good and Our Common Home

Focus for This Session

The needs of one are the needs of all in the human family.

Suggested Environment

On a small table, which may be decorated with the color of the liturgical season, you may have a Bible, a burning candle, and a crucifix, in addition to articles representative of the environment, such as water, stones, soil, or plant life.

Gather

Opening Prayer

Pray together:

Loving, gracious Creator God,
you have displayed a boundless love for all the world,
in all its height and depth and broad extent.

Especially in the vastness and beauty of the human species,
we recognize that we are so different and yet so much the same.

Forgive us for not seeing that your Spirit makes us one.

We separated ourselves from you because of rank, riches, and titles.

Mend our ways, O Lord. Help us to see that you intend for all of us only one common good: To live with you forever. Amen

Song Suggestion

"In This Place" (OCP)
Digital playlist available at www.renewintl.org/creation

Living Our Faith

Share briefly your experience of putting into effect the action you chose after the last session.

See: Farmers Learn Climate-Change Tactics

One of the youngest nations on the planet is Timor-Leste, or East Timor, which occupies half of an island midway between Indonesia and Australia. Although Timor-Leste is rich in natural resources and surrounded by sea life, it is one of the poorest countries in Southeast Asia.

This fragile country is vulnerable to the effects of a warming climate, not just because of rising temperatures and more violent storms but because its people—mostly subsistence farmers—depend on enough rain falling when it is needed and also on fertile soil that is not parched by drought or carried away by floods. The absence of these conditions threatens the food supply—crops and livestock—and the incomes of Timor-Leste people. Decreases in income have a ripple effect for people and the community including health care, education, and community cohesiveness.

Timorese teams operating under Caritas Australia, which is devoted to putting Catholic social teaching into action, have responded to these realities by helping many rural communities take steps to blunt the impact of climate change. These steps include farming methods and crop selection. In one of the poorest and most isolated of these communities, Oecusse, Caritas Australia helped establish a program in 16 schools, teaching students, teachers, and parents how to take better care of the environment.

Incencio Oki, a teacher at a primary school in Oecusse, said the program "teaches us to change our traditional practices if it helps the environment. Now we grow more trees, making terraces to avoid erosion, look after rubbish, and grow more plants in our local environment." Training also includes the use of organic fertilizers.

As parents and children learn together, the impact of this program reaches beyond the school to individual homes and gardens and, through the children, will reach succeeding generations, serving the common good in the present and for decades to come.

Source: *CaritasNews*, Spring 2015

The Word of God

Acts 4:32-35
Of One Heart and Mind

Moment of Silent Reflection

In light of the story about the effect of climate change on Timor-Leste, what word, phrase, or image from the scripture reading touched your heart or spoke to your life?

Invitation to Share

1. Share the word, phrase, or image from the scripture reading that touched your heart.

2. The early Christians described in the Acts of the Apostles promoted the common good by sharing their possessions, or selling them, so that everyone's needs were cared for. In your experience, where would you find evidence of such shared goodness as recounted in this scripture passage?

Reflection

At the core of Catholic social teaching is the understanding that each human being is created in the image and likeness of God and therefore possesses an inherent dignity and a status worthy of respect. However, we are not isolated agents but social by nature, reaching our full potential only in relationship with others, a concept that permeates *Laudato Si'* and is the basis for understanding the principle of the common good. The same idea is present in the sharing of goods as recounted in today's scripture passage. Caritas Australia and the Timorese teams that work under its auspices are contemporary examples of that idea in practice.

In his encyclical Pope Francis cites *Gaudium et Spes* (26), a document of the Second Vatican Council, which defined the common good as the "sum of those conditions of social life which allow social groups and their individual members to reach and to attain ready access to their own fulfillment." The word "fulfillment" implies certain rights, such as having food, clothing, housing, education, work, and respect. Fulfillment also includes rights to choose freely one's state in life, raise a family, enjoy one's good name, act according to the dictates of one's conscience, safeguard one's privacy, and practice religion. The pope also suggests that guaranteeing such rights does not require the establishment of new bureaucracies. Instead, he argues for "subsidiarity," reliance on a variety of intermediate groups—voluntary and private organizations, church groups, and especially, the family. That means that higher levels of authority, such as nations and international bodies, would step in only when lower levels could not carry out what is necessary for the common good (*Laudato Si'*, 157)

The common good also includes social peace, the stability and security provided by a certain order which cannot be achieved without concern for distributive justice. This type of justice ensures a basic equity in how both the burdens and the goods of society are distributed. When this is violated, crime and violence frequently ensue.

The pope writes further: "the principle of the common good is inevitably a summons to solidarity and a preferential option for the poorest of our brothers and sisters" (*Laudato Si'*, 158). The term "solidarity" in this context refers to a moral commitment to the welfare of others that goes beyond what justice requires. It's not just doing what duty and responsibility call for, but making the common good the foundation for moral action. The phrase "preferential option for the poor" means that the poor, the marginalized, and any persons whose living conditions interfere with their proper growth should be the focus of particular concern. An analogy might be the case of two children, one older and stronger, the other younger and physically weaker. The "preference" of the mother in a time of emergency would be to attend to the younger. The mother loves both children equally, but the younger and weaker would need more assistance. The passage from the Acts of the Apostles describes an early instance of a preferential option for the poor. The very existence of Caritas Australia and the work done by its staff and volunteers provide an example in our own time.

The term "common good" is not new, at least not in the social teaching of the Church. It has an ancient pedigree. In the fifth century B.C. Aristotle maintained that there were certain concerns so widely shared that the community was obliged to address them. The community was to take care of common defense, prosecute crime, and see to it that the marketplace operated fairly and for the benefit of all. The purpose of the community, in other words, was to create conditions that would allow its members to "reach their fulfillment." The concept, if not the term, of the common good permeates the teachings of Jesus and the rest of the New Testament. St.

Thomas Aquinas in the thirteenth century A.D. referred to the principle of the common good in his commentary on ethics.

Pope Leo XIII, in his 1891 encyclical *Rerum Novarum,* appealed to the conscience of the world regarding the rights and duties of labor. Working conditions were very difficult, especially in mines and factories, salaries were minimal, and safety was always an issue. Some moral guidelines were necessary. From that time until the present, popes have issued statements and encyclicals on a variety of social issues in the name of the global common good. So did the Second Vatican Council, which elucidated the concept of the common good in the pastoral constitution *On the Church in the Modern World* (*Gaudium et Spes*). Pope Francis, then, is not introducing a revolutionary idea; he is simply applying an historic principle to life in the modern world and to the ecological aspects of this traditional concept.

As we have already seen, the thinking of Pope Francis in this encyclical is based on the conviction of all creation having its source in Creator God. This type of thinking is always based on the relatedness and interconnectivity of all reality. Ethical behavior will always be related to community. It is behavior for the common good. Society as a whole, and the state in particular, are obliged to defend and promote the common good. But contemporary economic theory has created global economic systems that value "profit at any price" and a colonialist structure that reduces poor countries to mere providers of raw materials and cheap labor. Such systems lack that sober long-term thinking that comes with reflection on the common good.

> "We may well be leaving to coming generations debris, desolation and filth. The pace of consumption, waste and environmental change has so stretched the planet's capacity that our contemporary lifestyle, unsustainable as it is, can only precipitate catastrophes, such as those which even now periodically occur in different areas of the world. The effects of the present imbalance can only be reduced by our decisive action, here and now. We need to reflect on our accountability before those who will have to endure the dire consequences."
>
> Pope Francis, *Laudato Si'*, 161

The concept of the common good has clear ecological dimensions. People will not be able to flourish if the environment is so degraded that it loses its capacity to support life. Stated positively, a healthy environment is a precondition for human flourishing. People do not exist in a vacuum or bubble, apart from the environment around them. There is no common good without a healthy common home.

The notion of the common good also extends to future generations, an idea that takes flesh in the environmental training taking place in Timorese schools. This is not an optional matter but a basic question of justice. The created world which we have received and enjoyed also belongs to those who will follow us. The environment has been given to us as a "loan." We may have owned property and have used it with great care. But the property was here well before us, and it will remain when we are gone. It is God's gift, not to be used in some purely utilitarian, selfish, or destructive manner but with awareness that it was ultimately a loan. A sense of justice and self-respect calls us to pass it on to another generation with joy and pride.

What kind of a world do we want to leave to those who come after us? To our children? To our grandchildren? These are the underlying questions: What meaning and value do we give to the earth that has embraced us? What is the purpose of our lives? Why are we here? What is at stake here is our dignity, self-respect, and concern for those who will follow us. Leaving a sustainable planet for future generations is up to us. Will future generations be asking: Is this wasted planet all that they have left us? Didn't they foresee in their time what would become of our common home?

Invitation to Share

Take a few moments of silence to reflect on the following questions. Then share your reflections.

1. In what ways do you see our society implementing the principle of the common good?

2. In what ways do you see the notion of a "preferential option for the poor" practiced in your nation, town, or parish, or in your own life?

3. What kind of an environment would you want to leave for those who will come after you? Please give some examples.

Invitation to Act

Being together and sharing in a small Christian community fosters growth in our faith and in our spirituality. However, no communal sharing is complete without a serious commitment to putting our faith into practice. In this session we have reflected on the common good, the preferential option for the poor, and how both relate to care for creation. How does this inspire us to act? The following are examples.

1. Pope Francis ordered showers installed in Rome after learning that homeless people considered the lack of such facilities one of their greatest deprivations. Determine from local social service agencies what poor residents of your area are most in need of and work with your group or within your parish to address that need.

2. The concepts of integral environment and the common good both mean that the challenges facing people in remote places such as Timor-Leste are challenges for us, too. Discuss with your parish leadership how your parish might "adopt" a distant community by providing sustained assistance to help protect and restore the environment in that area— through tree planting, clean water projects, sustainable agricultural projects, or other forms of activity.

Closing Prayer

Pray together:

O God, let our longing for a healthy environment
be grounded in a confident awareness of your Spirit in our lives.

May that Spirit bless us with courage and hope
as we continue our humble efforts
to promote the care of the earth,
our common home, and to communicate our concern to others.

We thank you for gathering us together this day.
Bless the many who do not yet share the blessings of the common good.
Bless our families, friends, and loved ones.

Pause to allow members to ask for blessing on specific individuals or communities in need.

We ask this in the name of Jesus Christ, your Son,
who lives and reigns with you in the unity of the Holy Spirit,
one God, forever and ever. Amen.

Looking Ahead

Prepare for the next session by prayerfully reading

— Session 10, "Ecological Spirituality"

— Colossians 3:12-17

— Pope Francis's encyclical, *Laudato Si'*, paragraphs 202-215.

Learn More

Pope Francis' speech to the United Nations on Sept. 25, 2015;
http://w2.vatican.va/content/francesco/en/speeches/2015/
september/documents/papa-francesco_20150925_onu-visita.html

Compendium of the Social Doctrine of the Church,
http://www.vatican.va/roman_curia/pontifical_councils/justpeace/
documents/rc_pc_justpeace_doc_20060526_compendio-dott-
soc_en.html

Responses to 101 Questions on Catholic Social Teaching, Kenneth
R. Himes, OFM (Paulist Press)

"A great cultural, spiritual and educational challenge stands before us, and it will demand that we set out on the long path of renewal."

Pope Francis, *Laudato Si'*, 202

SESSION 10

Ecological Spirituality

Focus for This Session

Our relationships with each other and with the natural world are encounters with God.

Suggested Environment

On a small table, which may be decorated with the color of the liturgical season, you may have a Bible, a burning candle, and a crucifix, in addition to articles representative of the environment, such as water, stones, soil, or plant life.

Gather

Opening Prayer

Divide the group in two to pray the Canticle of St. Francis:

All: **Most High, all-powerful, good Lord,**
all praise is yours, all glory, all honor,
and all blessing.
To you, alone, Most High, do they belong.
No mortal lips are worthy to pronounce your name.

Side 1:	All praise be yours, my Lord, through all you have made, and first my lord Brother Sun, who brings the day; and through whom you give us light. How beautiful is he, how radiant in all his splendor; Of you, Most High, he bears the likeness.
Side 2:	All praise be yours, my Lord, through Sister Moon and the stars; in the heavens you have made them, bright, and precious, and fair.
Side 1:	All praise be yours, my Lord, through Brothers Wind and Air, and fair and stormy, all the weather's moods, by which you cherish all that you have made.
Side 2:	All praise be yours, my Lord, through Sister Water, so useful, humble, precious and pure.
Side 1:	All praise be yours, my Lord, through Brother Fire, through whom you brighten up the night. How beautiful is he, how cheerful! Full of power and strength.
Side 2:	All praise be yours, my Lord, through our Sister, Mother Earth, who sustains us and governs us, and produces various fruits with colored flowers and herbs.
Side 1:	All praise be yours, my Lord, through those who grant pardon for love of you; through those who endure sickness and trial. Happy are those who endure in peace, By You, Most High, they will be crowned.
All:	**All praise be yours, my Lord, through Sister Death, From whose embrace no mortal can escape. Woe to those who die in mortal sin! Happy those she finds doing your will! The second death can do them no harm. Praise and bless my Lord, and give him thanks And serve him with great humility.**

Song Suggestion

"God Beyond All Names" (OCP)
Digital playlist available at www.renewintl.org/creation

Living Our Faith

Share briefly your experience of putting into effect the action you chose after the last session.

See: Our "Stuff" Can Overwhelm Us

What is a garage? The obvious answer is that it's a place to park a car, but some research shows that most garages are not used for that purpose.

Instead, according to an intensive study of 24 families over four full days in 2001, some 75 percent of garages were too full of possessions spilling over from the house.

The study was conducted, among two-income middle-class households in Los Angeles, by archaeologists, anthropologists, and other social scientists affiliated with UCLA's Center on Everyday Lives of Families. These were a few more of the findings:

— The increase in large "big box" retail stores results in a greater tendency to accumulate consumer products in already overburdened space.

— Large master bedroom-bathroom suites were the most common alterations to the homes, but the space was hardly ever used.

— Families seldom used the outdoor part of their property for leisure, even if they had spent money enhancing it—and this in a region with nice weather all year.

— Increased stress hormones in women in particular could be correlated with the challenge of managing a home so crowded with material possessions.

Source: "Trouble in paradise: UCLA book enumerates challenges faced by middle-class L.A. families," http://newsroom.ucla.edu, June 19, 2012.

The Word of God

Colossians 3:12-17
Called to Peace in One Body

Moment of Silent Reflection

In light of the study on middle-class families in Los Angeles, what word, phrase, or image from St. Paul's letter touched your heart or spoke to you personally?

Invitation to Share

1. Share the word, phrase, or image from the scripture reading that touched your heart.

2. St. Paul's letter to the Colossians emphasizes the unity that was essential to the Christian community. As you join others in the worship and work of your parish, in what ways are you conscious of this unity? In what ways can you help to build it?

Reflection

Paul's letter to the Colossians, written toward the middle of the first century A.D., speaks to a Christian community undergoing change and development. With the passing of another generation, Paul is trying to transfer the genuine meaning and legacy of Jesus Christ by reminding his followers that they are now the Body of Christ. They are now to "put on," or to clothe themselves, with the garb appropriate to members of such a community.

In a similar manner, more than two thousand years later, Pope Francis writes to Catholics, and to all people of good faith, about issues pertaining to the relationship between our endangered environment and Christian faith and practice. In the final chapter of his encyclical *Laudato Si'*, he presents an "ecological spirituality" that will give direction to the Body of Christ. What values do we want to guide us into the future? In both instances, Paul, the Apostle to the Gentiles, and Francis, the 266th pope, offer time-proven guidelines.

The final chapter of Pope Francis's encyclical on ecology is a call to moral and spiritual discernment and, more specifically, a call for education in ecological spirituality. As mentioned above, the "realities of education," as they develop into habits, attitudes, and virtues, will eventually become evangelical practices.

The challenge is very clear in his opening words in the final chapter: "Many things have to change course, but it is we human beings above all who need to change. We lack an awareness of our common origin, of our mutual belonging, and of a future to be shared with everyone" (202). Certain attitudes and actions endemic to consumer capitalism and mentioned throughout the encyclical will make changing course difficult for many: compulsive consumerism, self-centeredness leading to greed, unwillingness to accept limits, unrestrained shopping, absence of any sense of the common good. Yet all is not lost. We are still capable of responding to God's grace at work in our hearts. We are still capable of going out of ourselves towards the other. If we can overcome individualism, we will truly be able to develop a new life style, new habits, and new actions, which lead to authentic human life.

The goals of environmental education have been broadened. In the beginning there was more focus on scientific information, awareness of environmental risks. Now there is far more emphasis on trying to change behaviors, attitudes, and social structures in order to establish harmony within ourselves, with others, with nature, with other living creatures, and with God. This kind of education encourages a reach towards the transcendent, which gives ecological ethics its deepest meaning. Its focus is not simply information but good habits and personal and social transformation, which lead to the development of virtues that enable people to make selfless and conscious commitments. At times, these commitments may appear in simple, ordinary actions such as reducing water consumption, separating refuse, cooking only what can be reasonably consumed, using public transport or pooling cars, or turning off unnecessary lights. At other times, these commitments may feel new or challenging, such as the need to become involved in local, regional or national political processes or social movements to advocate for policy changes that will create a healthy environment for our children. These efforts together, carried out by many, many people, are what is needed to address climate change and the other major environmental challenges we face. When we take action, individually and collectively, we will both foster and reveal an inner consciousness of caring for the earth. Such efforts call forth goodness that inevitably tends to spread.

> **"Disinterested concern for others, and the rejection of every form of self-centeredness and self-absorption, are essential if we truly wish to care for our brothers and sisters and for the natural environment. These attitudes also attune us to the moral imperative of assessing the impact of our every action and personal decision on the world around us. If we can overcome individualism, we will truly be able to develop a different lifestyle and bring about significant changes in society."**
>
> Pope Francis, *Laudato Si'*, 208

Ecological education can take place in a variety of settings. In the family, we first learn how to show love and respect for life. The family is the heart of the culture of life. In the family we receive an integral education, which enables us to grow into maturity in harmony with the world around us. Other settings such as the church, school, certain forms of media, and Christian catechesis can provide fertile ground for the young to grow and to continue bearing good fruit throughout life.

Ecological education also consists of being at peace with oneself. Peace is not simply the absence of war. Peace, in its biblical roots is "shalom," the wholeness of relationships. It is closely related to care for the environment, because when lived authentically it is reflected in a balanced lifestyle. It provides an inner harmony that counters frenetic activity. Such peace is from within. It sets the stage for a sense of awe, wonder, and reverence for the sacredness of life. We are then in a position to contemplate the Creator who lives among us and surrounds us. When we experience such peace, we've got to share it with others. We become a universal fraternity; we share a responsibility for one another and for the world around us.

Within the Christian tradition, an ecological and spiritual education that speaks of such togetherness also speaks about the sacraments, especially the Eucharist. The sacraments are a privileged way in which nature is taken up by God and becomes a way of mediating God's life. Pouring water over a baby's head in baptism, anointing a sick person's forehead and hands, praying the words of reconciliation, "Your sins are forgiven, go in peace"—these are all signs and symbols of God's powerful love. They are not magic, nor are they divine in themselves, but they are signs of God's presence. For Christians, all creatures of the material universe find true meaning in the Incarnate Word. The Son of God has taken on human flesh; in his person he takes on a part of the human world, planting in it a seed of definitive transformation.

It is in the Eucharist, however, that creation finds its greatest exaltation. Grace is expressed in a tangible way. God gives himself as food for all, choosing to reach our depths through fragments of matter, bread and wine shared in a community of faith. God does not come from above but from within many different forms of creation. Consider what is needed to make the "fruits of the earth and of the vine" into the Body and Blood of Christ. The Eucharist does not happen without seeds, soil, sun, water, and all of nature's processes that foster growth. To break bread at the eucharistic table also calls for a farmer to plant and cultivate the wheat, to fertilize and harvest it. The miller grinds it into flour; the baker bakes it, before it is ready to be eaten by the community. A similar process takes place with regard to growing, harvesting, and preparing the grapes for wine.

The world, which came from God's hands, returns to him in the bread and wine, the body and blood, of the eucharistic table. Pope Francis cites the words of his predecessor, Pope Benedict XVI: "Creation is projected towards divinization, towards the holy wedding feast, towards unification with the Creator himself" (236). The works of creation, bread and wine, are transformed into the Body of Christ. It is this body that continues to give praise and witness to God. Indeed, the Eucharist itself is an act of cosmic love.

Our participation in the Sunday Eucharist has special importance. Like the Jewish Sabbath, it is meant to restore our relationship with God, ourselves, and those communities that give us life. The quality time that is to be spent with our friends and loved ones on Sunday calls us to slow down and to be at rest. Such use of time should not be considered wasted, unnecessary, or meaningless. Time and rest are needed for healing and restoration. We are not automatons; our bodies and minds grow weary. Actually, we work so that we may have the time to renew our relationships and to refresh our bodies. To offset the rapid pace and frenetic activity of life, it is also necessary to honor the contemplative part of the human person. Our inner spirit also needs to be reanimated.

Pope Francis concludes his summons to an ecological spirituality by invoking the Blessed Trinity. He writes, "For Christians, believing in one God who is trinitarian communion suggests that the Trinity has left its mark on all of creation" (*Laudato Si'*, 239). Created according to the dynamic model of Trinity, as three in one, the world is a web of relationships. To be is to be in relationship. We grow toward fulfillment and meaning in life to the extent that we grow in communion with God, with others and with all of creation. Everything is inter-connected and this invites us to a spirituality of that global solidarity which flows from the mystery of the Trinity.

Invitation to Share

Take a few moments of silence to reflect on the following questions. Then share your reflections.

1. What helps you to remember that God, rather than being a figure off in the distance, is present in every particle of the world he creates?

2. The reflections in this book have referred to a "ecological spirituality," using a term (spirituality) that we often associate with an invisible world. What would it mean to you to embrace a spirituality focused not on an unseen heaven but on the visible, touchable world of everyday life?

3. How can you make the celebration of Sunday more of a "greening experience," one that lifts up these seen revelations of God in our world?

Invitation to Act

Being together and sharing in a small Christian community fosters growth in our faith and in our spirituality. However, no communal sharing is complete without a serious commitment to putting our faith into practice. In this session we have reflected on ecological spirituality. How does this inspire us to act? The following are examples.

1. Talk to your parish leadership team about conducting a survey to identify individuals or families in your community who because of age or financial limitations are unable to care for their homes and property. Organize a team of adults and teenagers to offer to help with this work.

2. Reduce your use of disposable products by using reusable containers; if you must buy disposable, buy paper or glass products instead of plastic. If you order take-out meals, decline the plastic utensils that are usually offered. Consider the same practices of reducing plastic and disposable products within your parish hall for after-Mass events or other social events.

3. Traditional firewood and charcoal stoves, commonly used in developing countries, emit black carbon or soot as the result of incomplete combustion during cooking. The carbon not only affects the environment but is also a big health risk, particularly dangerous for women and children who spend long hours in the kitchen. Organize a fundraiser in your parish to sponsor the purchase of fuel-efficient cookstoves for a village of people in a developing country. Such cookstoves can provide safe drinking water, conserve fuel, and reduce indoor air pollution.

4. Inquire at the headquarters of your local government about what agencies and organizations are responsible for protecting and restoring the environment. Identify groups that are working to change policies that determine the quality of the environment. Find out how you might get involved.

5. Make the canticle of St. Francis a part of your daily spiritual regimen.

Closing Prayer

Divide the group in two in order to recite the following prayer:

Group 1:   Gracious, loving Creator God,
                we thank you for the bounty of this generous earth
                we call our common home.

Group 2:   We thank you for the change of seasons with their many
                miracles of transformation.

Group 1:   We thank you for the trees, the flowers and plants, and the
                grass under our feet.

Group 2:   We thank you for the many signs of your Spirit
              abundant in our lives.

Group 1:   All praise be yours, my Lord, through Brother Fire,
              through whom you brighten up the night.
              How beautiful is he, how cheerful!
              Full of power and strength.

Group 2:   We thank you for the gift of one another,
              for the friendships that sustain us.

All: **May the graciousness of Mother Earth**
              in all of its myriad forms
              make of our own lives an expression
              of praise and glory to your name. Amen.

Looking Ahead

Prepare for the next session by prayerfully reading

— Session 11, "Ecological Conversion: We Need a Change of Heart"

— Luke 3:7-14

— Pope Francis's encyclical, *Laudato Si'*, paragraphs 216-227.

Learn More

GreenFaith's GreenWorship resource offers an array of prayers
and resources to help integrate environmental care into your
parish liturgies: **http://www.greenfaith.org/resource-center/spirit/**
greenworship-resource/christian-resource-1/christian-resource

"The ecological crisis is a summons to profound interior conversion… whereby the effects of our encounter with Jesus Christ becomes evident in our relationship with the world around us."

Pope Francis, *Laudato Si'*, 217

Ecological Conversion: We Need a Change of Heart

Focus for This Session

Renewal of our common home requires conversion of individual hearts and of society.

Suggested Environment

On a small table, which may be decorated with the color of the liturgical season, you may have a Bible, a burning candle, and a crucifix, in addition to articles representative of the environment, such as water, stones, soil, or plant life.

Gather

Opening Prayer

Pray together:

**Loving, gracious Creator God,
in former times, you called upon the prophets
to challenge your people to change their ways,
to be converted, and to return to covenant love.**

**You reminded us again through John the Baptist
to mend our ways, to experience conversion of mind and heart.**

**In that spirit we repent for the ways in which we have failed to protect
and care for the world you have given us.
We pray that your Spirit may inspire and motivate us
to renew the face of the earth.**

We ask this through Jesus Christ, our Lord. Amen.

Song Suggestion

"Change Our Hearts" (OCP)
Digital playlist available at www.renewintl.org/creation

Living Our Faith

Share briefly your experience of putting into effect the action you chose after the last session.

See: "Super Storm" Creates a Leader

Grace and her husband happily raised their family in a lovely house at the New Jersey shore. The night in 2012 that Hurricane Sandy struck, they were home. They had decided not to evacuate. After all, they had ridden out numerous storms and hurricanes. Then they saw the seven-foot surge wave barreling toward their home. The water rose quickly in the house. The sump pumps struggled non-stop; soon oil from the furnace began to leak heavily. The house was flooded with a thick mix of water and oil. The family survived. The house did not. Three years later the house and land were still contaminated.

"That night my life changed forever," says Grace. Over time, she began to look for a deeper meaning in her terrifying and heartbreaking experience. The support of a loving church community gave her strength and insight. She turned to prayer and meditation. She was grateful that her family had survived. The repeated nightmares of the dark, oily mixture gradually gave way to dreams of peacefully flowing clean water.

"I changed," she says. Prior to Sandy, she had been vaguely conscious of the environment and of climate change in particular. She began to study the causes of global warming. She, once again, fell in love with the ocean. In her prayer and meditation, her reading and conversations, and her discovery of local efforts to protect the environment, she began to see that "We are all connected to everything. We are one."

Grace passionately felt called to "make a difference." Today, she is involved in water and climate issues, working with groups that are making a difference by trying to create laws and policies needed to protect our common home.

The Word of God

Luke 3:7-14
Produce Good Fruits

Moment of Silent Reflection

In light of the story about Grace's conversion, what word, phrase, or image from the scripture reading touched your heart or spoke to your life?

Invitation to Share

1. Share the word, phrase, or image from the scripture reading that touched your heart.

2. John the Baptist prepared the way for Jesus. How does his witness, as recorded by Luke, help you live according to the Gospel of Jesus Christ?

Reflection

Running through Pope Francis' encyclical is a call to ecological conversion. This must take place first on a personal level, as in the case of Grace. But to have any lasting effects, conversion must also occur on a community level. Conversion is a passionate conviction about a spirituality that will inspire and lead people to action on personal and communal levels. This kind of spirituality cannot be dissociated from the earth or the body. To say "the Word became flesh" (incarnation) is to say that Jesus was born of matter, having a body like ours. Both divine and human, he was closely connected with other human beings and with his environment. The state of the environment, then, is not simply an economic, technical, or political issue, but also a religious and spiritual affair. A spirituality of conversion begins with the confession that human beings are the primary cause of the world's environmental crises. But we have not always recognized or acknowledged that we have harmed God's creation through our actions or through our failure to act. For example, the fact that we humans are consuming more resources than the earth can produce may not be clear to many people. In fact, some dismiss that fact with a casual statement such as "God will provide; Mother Nature is very generous!" However, we are consuming natural resources beyond the earth's capacity to regenerate them, and that amounts to stealing from future generations.

A change in awareness and attitude and a commitment to action are necessary. Repentance from environmental sin demands a new way of viewing our world and living in it. We live in this world not simply as isolated individuals but as vital parts of the community of creation. Pope Francis writes that a "healthy relationship with creation … entails the recognition of our sins, faults, and failures, and leads to heartfelt repentance and desire to change" (218). Such desire calls for profound inner conversion.

"Conversion" here means change, transformation, or more literally a "turning around" of one's attitudes of mind and heart, a change of behavior. It is a new way of discerning life on the basis of a personal religious conviction. The underlying Greek word *metanoia* signifies a radical turning around of the whole person and a returning home. The comparable Hebrew term from the Old Testament, *shub*, speaks of a turning away from pagan idols and returning to the values of the covenant God. For some, "repentance" may evoke a sense of guilt for sins that some people consider insignificant. Repentance, however, means more than a resolve to avoid transgression of law; it also means a commitment to actions of mercy, justice, and compassion. Such is the meaning of John the Baptist's words in the scriptural passage above. When those in the crowd asked him, "What must we do [to experience conversion]?" he challenged them to a genuine *metanoia*, a "turning around" of their lives, evident in actions of justice and mercy, not simply resolutions.

> "Nature is filled with words of love, but how can we listen to them amid constant noise, interminable and nerve-wracking distractions, or the cult of appearances? Many people today sense a profound imbalance which drives them to frenetic activity and makes them feel busy, in a constant hurry which in turn leads them to ride rough-shod over everything around them. This too affects how they treat the environment."
>
> Pope Francis, *Laudato Si'*, 225

Conversion is not a one-time experience. It is an ongoing process, gradual, and frequently arduous. Ecological conversion involves a series of "turnings," either away from our disregard for or exploitation of Mother Earth or a "turning" to a more authentic way of living in harmony with the earth. Whenever the grace of genuine conversion takes place, it presupposes a deep and honest relationship with God, with others, with the world around us.

There are various levels of ecological conversion. These "turnings" may be different one from another, but they all are interrelated:

1. The primary turn is toward God. Grace makes our hearts turn away from evil and return to God. "Restore us to yourself, O Lord, that we may be restored" (Lamentations 5:21). Pope Francis encourages praying for the conversion of the heart. He suggests something as ordinary as saying a prayer before every meal. That brief moment reminds us of our dependence on the God of life. It strengthens our feeling of gratitude for the gifts of creation and for those who labor to provide those gifts, and reaffirms our solidarity with those in greatest need.

2. We turn also toward other people. No one of us is an island. Knowing that we are inextricably bound to one another leads to a maturity of interdependence. We realize that we differ from one another in many ways and yet are all made in the image and likeness of God. In others, we will see the face of God, as they too see God in us. In allowing others to be what they are, we allow ourselves to be more completely who we are. Such a relationship is the basis for mutual respect and a greater appreciation for one another's dignity.

3. Turning to the beauty and mystery of the earth around us, whether in a beautiful sunset, a snow-capped mountain, or even a polluted landscape, is a profound step in our conversion of heart. Nature is filled with words of love, and also of pain due to our mistreatment or misuse. As Pope Francis writes, "the earth and the poor cry out to us." If we never slow down to listen, to embrace the softening rhythms of creation, we will not be able to experience the sacred in our midst. To be in God's indwelling and transcendent presence, evokes reverence, awe and wonder, the prelude to "ecological prayer." We need such moments of quiet to experience our place in the circle of life.

4. When we turn and take a good, honest look at ourselves, we should be able to examine our own conscience: Are we lessening our own practices of consumerism? Are we shopaholics, spending freely on what we don't really need? Do we realize that purchasing is always a moral—and not simply an economic—act? Do we waste food? Do we use water in excess? Are we trying to lead a simple life, or are we simply living? Have we become involved in efforts to change the sinful systems that produce environmental degradation? The point is not to inspire guilt but to make us more aware of how each of us can contribute, even in small ways, to regenerating our common home.

As Pope Francis reminds us, "Self-improvement on the part of individuals will not itself remedy the complex situation facing the world today" (*Laudato*

Si', 219). The larger challenge is the transformation of social structures which cannot be accomplished at a single time or by any one individual. Rather, ecological conversion has to be viewed developmentally as a constant striving for a "new creation" that is experienced most effectively when done in communion with those of similar mind and heart.

We are heartened by the change that took place in Grace after she survived the destruction of her home in Hurricane Sandy. Now she feels passionately about "making a difference," working with environmental groups. Conversion of society begins with individuals like her. Individuals begin meeting with other groups, and the message spreads. Groups that gather to share the news of *Laudato Si'* eventually become empowered to reach out to larger structures of society. The major political and economic challenges outlined in other parts of the encyclical will never be met without the widespread personal and community conversion to which Pope Francis calls us.

Letters to the Editor

Despite the rapid evolution of newspaper companies into multimedia companies, the old-fashioned "letter to the editor" is still an effective means of expressing your opinion or calling attention to a problem regarding the environment. Although print circulation has drastically declined, most newspaper companies have web sites where letters to the editor, if anything, can get wider exposure than ever. And those who are interested in public opinion, including government officials and their staffs, will seek out the letters in order to keep in touch with public opinion.

Before writing or sending a letter, check the website or newspaper for the correct address and for any guidelines regarding acceptable letters. In general, keep your letter brief; most publications limit letters to 150-175 words. Be as factual as possible, and be careful with spelling and grammar; remember that the letter may be edited for length, grammar, and accuracy, and it's in your interest to have the letter published as closely as possible to the way you wrote it.

Include your full name, home address, and telephone number in case the editor wants to verify that you sent the letter or has questions about it.

Invitation to Share

Take a few moments of silence to reflect on the following questions. Then share your reflections.

1. When and how did you first become aware of the importance of ecology and your role in it? How has your awareness evolved over time?

2. Where do you recognize opportunities for a genuine change of mind and heart, with respect to the environment, in your own household or at your workplace?

3. How is your attitude toward the physical world affected by your faith that, in Jesus, God took on human form and lived in our common home?

Invitation to Act

Being together and sharing in a small Christian community fosters growth in our faith and in our spirituality. However, no communal sharing is complete without a serious commitment to putting our faith into practice. In this session we have reflected on the need for conversion as it relates to ecology. How does this inspire us to act? The following are examples.

1. Determine and put in place the steps needed to carry out the environmental principle "reduce, reuse, recapture" in your home, your school, or your workplace.

2. Research and share with your group, your family, and your friends, guidance for making the best ecological choices when making large purchases such as home appliances, a car, or even a home.

3. Become part of local or regional efforts to protect the environment through changing laws and regulations.

4. Research the availability and cost-effectiveness of using solar power or other renewable energy choices that may be offered by your local electric utility to provide electricity to your home. Share this information with your neighbors.

Closing Prayer

Pray together:

Gracious, loving Creator God,
you have summoned us at various times and in different ways:
"Return to me with contrite mind and heart, and know that I am
your God."

But so often we have been blind to the presence of your grace,
and deaf to the promptings of your Spirit.
Forgive our waywardness.

May we experience the gift of true repentance and renewal,
so that we might experience once again your loving presence.

We ask this through our Lord Jesus Christ. Amen.

Looking Ahead

Prepare for the next session by prayerfully reading

— Session 12, "Caring for Our Common Home"

— Matthew 7:24-27

— Pope Francis's encyclical, *Laudato Si'*, paragraphs 228-246.

"I urgently appeal for a new dialogue about how we are shaping the future of our planet. We need a conversation which includes everyone, since the environmental challenge we are undergoing, and its human roots, concern and affect all of us."

Pope Francis, Laudato Si', 14

SESSION 12

Caring for our Common Home

Focus for This Session

The encyclical on care of our common home calls us to be "doers of the word."

Suggested Environment

On a small table, which may be decorated with the color of the liturgical season, you may have a Bible, a burning candle, and a crucifix, in addition to articles representative of the environment, such as water, stones, soil, or plant life.

Gather

Opening Prayer

Divide the group in two to pray the following:

Leader:	Gracious, loving Creator God, you have formed us out of the earth and breathed into us the breath of life.
Group 1:	You have endowed us with an inner light to grow, prosper, and care for this earth.

Group 2:   Through your Son, Jesus, you have shown us the way to truth
            and fullness of life.

Group 1:   We pray in and through the Spirit of your Son
            for the courage to believe
            that nothing is beyond our collective ability
            to dream of a better world,
            trusting that our dreams can be turned into actions
            of care for creation.

Group 2:   May these dreams be built not on sand but on the solid
            foundation of loving effort.

All: **May it be so, Lord; may it be so. Amen.**

Song Suggestion

"The Church's One Foundation" (OCP)
Digital playlist available at www.renewintl.org/creation

Living Our Faith

*Share briefly your experience of putting into effect the action you chose after the
last session.*

See: "God Needs Everyone to Preserve His Creation"

Fr. Larry Schanberger was a Maryknoll missioner serving the parish of
Our Lady of Mercy in Puente Alto, Chile. As an ecological effort and to
beautify the grounds of his parish, he hoped to plant thirty liquidambar
or "sweetgum" trees in the vacant areas surrounding the church. He sent
invitations to thirty families he thought might be interested in this endeavor.
To his delight, thirty families signed up. But would they come?

On the cold, rainy morning of planting day, twenty-six families arrived
with shovels, name tags, and an eagerness to plant their trees. Father Larry
trusted that Our Lady of Mercy would not let him down. He sent the families
forth with encouragement to continue to care for God's creation. When
the planters returned, wet and dirty, they smiled broadly because they had
accomplished their tasks.

After celebratory cups of hot chocolate, he gave each family a certificate
honoring them as members of the "Liquidambar Tree Club." Then he made
one request: "Before you leave, please answer this question in writing: 'Why
did you come on this bleak Saturday morning to plant a tree?'" The responses
that follow indicate the quality of these Chilean people and what they deem
important for the earth.

"I love God's beautiful world, and I want to preserve it. I want to help our planet breathe better."

"It's a new beginning for personal growth and the growth of my family."

"God needs everyone to preserve his creation, and our action is like a grain of sand by which we contribute to the nature of our planet."

"I want to continue growing with Christ and in Christ, and I think that with this tree, that purifies and cleanses, I am heading in the right direction."

"We must teach our children by example the importance of caring for God's creation."

"I did not decide to plant a tree. It was God who permitted me to participate in caring for his creation."

Father Larry wondered if those families would come. Not only did they come, but they gave a beautiful lesson about caring for creation, our common home. The parish of Our Lady of Mercy in Puente Alto, Chile, is built on solid foundations. The ecological witness of its parishioners is not one of words alone but of action.

The Word of God

Matthew 7:24-27
Act on the Words of the Gospel

Moment of Silent Reflection

In light of the story about Our Lady of Mercy Parish, what word, phrase, or image from the scripture reading touched your heart or spoke to your life?

Invitation to Share

1. Share the word, phrase, or image from the scripture reading that touched your heart.

2. Describe an instance in which you made a decision or took an action because of what you heard and believed in the Gospel?

Reflection

Now that we have reflected on the central themes in Pope Francis' encyclical, *Laudato Si'*, we are left with this challenge: "Be doers of the word, not just hearers!" This challenge is stated very clearly in Pope Francis' apostolic exhortation, *The Joy of the Gospel*, where he writes, "Not to put the word into practice, not to make it a reality, is to build on sand; the word will remain in the realm of pure ideas, and end up in lifeless and unfruitful self-centeredness." This encyclical is not meant to be a mere compendium of ideas. It is meant to be acted upon. It should become fruitful and life-giving. So important is this principle of acting upon the word and making it a reality that Pope Francis sees it as a way of experiencing the incarnation in our own era—God come to flesh anew in works of evangelization and actions of justice and charity (*The Joy of the Gospel*, 233).

This final reflection of *Creation at the Crossroads* is meant to offer practical and pastoral examples of putting into practice the ideals of the encyclical. The purpose is to continue the conversation but also to translate it into effective actions regarding care for our common home. Inevitably, beginning such a process raises certain questions: How do we begin? What do we do? Whom do we consult? What should we be reading? Who will lead us? The answers to these questions will differ greatly, depending on the circumstances, resources, motivation, and leadership of each individual or group. Through the suggested actions following each of the previous eleven sessions, you already have a great start. What follows is a simplified initial procedure that focuses on the establishment of a parish environment committee (PEC). This model is meant to be flexible, not "chipped in stone." It is based on the author's five years of experience with a parish environmental committee that is thriving and growing and, in fact, has received renewed energy with the publication of the encyclical *Laudato Si'*.

From the beginning, there is a need to recognize the importance of three P's: prayer, patience, and perseverance. As nature needs time to produce bountiful growth, so does a parish environmental committee need time to set down roots, grow, and mature. The following points also should be borne in mind:

> "Society is ... enriched by a countless array of organizations which work to promote the common good and to defend the environment, whether natural or urban. ... Thus, a community can break out of the indifference induced by consumerism. These actions cultivate a shared identity, with a story which can be remembered and handed on. In this way, the world, and the quality of life of the poorest, are cared for, with a sense of solidarity which is at the same time aware that we live in a common home which God has entrusted to us. These community actions, when they express self-giving love, can also become intense spiritual experiences."
>
> Pope Francis, *Laudato Si'*, 232

— Getting authorization from the pastor or administrator is an important first step. As the shepherd of the community, he provides the approval, cooperation, and resources of the entire parish community to support the efforts of your fledgling PEC.

— A temporary leader should arrange for an invitation to the entire parish to attend an opening meeting for those interested in participating in a PEC. Ideally, those who have already taken part in the *Creation at the Crossroads* process will be interested in following up on what they talked about and prayed about in their small groups. The basic purpose of this initial meeting would be sharing ideas, allowing people to vocalize their hopes for and opinions about the project. Each parish has its own unique context (urban, rural, suburban, farming, coastal) which will shape the discussion. Once the key topics of discussion are recorded, the group should prioritize them for further discussion at the next meeting. Before the introductory session concludes, a committee should be formed to continue the planning process and also to determine the time and place of the next meeting.

— This next meeting of the PEC involves a review of the prioritized points from the opening meeting in order to prepare a preliminary mission statement. The task will be to answer, in a few clearly stated sentences, these questions: Why are we establishing a PEC in this parish? What do we want to accomplish? How will this committee be of benefit to our parish and our community? At this stage, the mission statement will be provisional. How to actually accomplish this mission, the need for objectives, and formation of sub-committees to take on specific tasks will come afterwards. Depending on circumstances, this step may require more than one meeting. Also, by this stage, participants should agree on a name for the PEC.

— The next step, a crucial one, is to gather the active and interested PEC members for a more extended period of prayer and reflection—one full day, or even an overnight if possible. In this retreat-like context, it would be very helpful to have an experienced facilitator. Such a person can provide additional insights into the discussions, as well as the expertise to help in the formulation of a final mission statement. At this point, it will be very important to focus more precisely on that area of the environment which is most important to the parish, given its particular setting. Will it be the question of energy, clean water, air pollution, sustainable resources, food, waste management, overfishing? Choosing a focus for environmental action in the community will provide direction to all activities concerning the PEC.

For example, the PEC on which these reflections are based chose the issue of sustainability/agriculture and food. As a first step, the group decided to start a parish community garden. The initiation of this project generated more interest, more volunteers, and a further set of objectives that included opportunities within the parish for education on ecology and a structure for providing fresh produce from the garden to those in need. In keeping with Pope Francis' appeal for solidarity and preferential action for the poor, our parish has now broadened its connection with other people in need.

In addition to actions by individuals or by groups such as a PEC, advocacy—responsibly directed at government, businesses, and industries— for repairing and protecting the environment is urgently needed. Pope Francis mentions often in his encyclical that none of us can do this work alone. We need to collaborate with, and sometimes challenge, agencies and individuals about the importance of caring for our common home.

And one thing paramount for any person or group devoted to protecting the earth is prayer, and especially the celebration of the Eucharist. It is within the liturgical context of the eucharistic community that we are reminded of the sacredness of the earth in the elements of bread and wine that come to us from the soil, sun, rain, and the work of many human hands. Other opportune times for involving the entire parish are celebrations of the seasons, Earth Day, and the feast of St. Francis with the blessing of animals. Where appropriate, para-liturgical celebrations—such as processions and special days of prayer for blessing of fields, first fruits, and harvested produce—are ways of celebrating the sacredness and bounty of the earth. And frequent recitation of the canticle of St. Francis will remind us of how related we are to Brother Sun and Sister Moon and to all of God's creation. "All praise be yours, my Lord, for all that you have made. Amen."

Invitation to Share

Take a few moments of silence to reflect on the following questions. Then share your reflections.

1. In what way could you be a "doer of God's word," in addition to being a "hearer of God's word," when it comes to caring for the earth?

2. In what way would an environmental committee be practical in your parish or organization?

3. What is the major environmental concern in your area? How is that concern related to your life and the lives of your family?

Invitation to Act

Being together and sharing in a small Christian community fosters growth in our faith and in our spirituality. However, no communal sharing is complete without a serious commitment to putting our faith into practice. In this session we have reflected on the need to be "doers of the word" with regard to Laudato Si'. *How does this inspire us to act? The following are examples.*

1. Ask your pastor about the feasibility of establishing a parish environmental committee (PEC).

2. Urge the people you regularly interact with, Catholic or not, to read Pope Francis' encyclical and then engage them in conversation about how the letter affected them. Let them know about what you as an individual or your parish is doing to care for our common home, and invite them to play a part.

3. Keep current on events that impact the earth. Create and maintain an up-to-date list of contact information for public officials who represent you on the local, state or provincial, and national levels, and write to them regularly about environmental issues that come to your attention.

4. Take advantage of opportunities to write letters for publication in newspapers and on their web sites, calling attention to problems affecting the environment in your community or in the wider world.

Closing Prayer

Pray together:

O God, Creator of all that is, give us light and strength to know your will, to make it our own, and to live it in our lives.

Help us to be good stewards of the treasures of your creation: living persons, animals and plants, rivers and forests, lands and seas. As we strive to be faithful caretakers of our common home, help us always to be, not only hearers of your word, but also doers. May our humble efforts always be built not on sand but on the solid rock of our commitment to value and protect what you have made. We ask this through Jesus Christ, your Son, who lives and reigns with you, in the unity of the Holy Spirit, one God, forever and ever. Amen.

Learn More

To learn how to make your parish or community's food choices more sustainable: **http://www.greenfaith.org/resource-center/ stewardship/food-and-faith**

GreenFaith's Shield Programs offer parishes and faith communities a weekend-long program to reduce their energy and water use, and to equip their members to do the same: **http://www.greenfaith.org/ programs/greenfaith-shield**

For faith communities ready for a true creation-care makeover, GreenFaith's Certification Program offers a truly transformational opportunity to integrate environmental care into worship, religious education, facility management, social concerns, and more: **http://www.greenfaith.org/programs/certification**

GreenFaith's on-line resource library offers resources to help faith communities deepen their spirituality and worship in relation to God's creation, to manage their facilities in a greener manner, and to advocate for a healthy environment for those who are most vulnerable: **http://www.greenfaith.org/resource-center**

Looking Back, Looking Ahead ...

Looking Back ...

— Reflecting on your experience with *Creation at the Crossroads,* share as a group:

1. What has touched your heart?

2. What experiences have helped you grow as a person and as a community? Why?

3. How has faith sharing moved you to live out the Gospel in a new way by taking steps to protect and preserve the environment?

— Provide input to your small-community leader, including photos of your small community in action.

— Send Good News stories and pictures regarding steps your group or parish took to protect or advocate for our common home to goodnews@renewintl.org

Looking Ahead ...

— Stay connected.

— Pray for and stay in touch with each other.

— Encourage one another to participate in parish outreach efforts.

— Read our inspirational reflections at blog.renewintl.org.

— "Like" us at Facebook.com/RENEWintl.

— Subscribe to the World RENEW enewsletter at www.renewintl.org/subscribe.

Keep it Going

— Continue to faith share all year round. See RENEW International's resources beginning on page 122.

— View and discuss *Turning Points: Witness Stories,* a RENEW video series at youtube.com/TurningPointsStories.

— Share your experience of *Creation at the Crossroads* with friends and family.

Appendix

A Hindu Response to *Laudato Si'*

By Shanuaka Rishi Das

The Roman Catholic encyclical, *Laudato Si'* (*On Care for Our Common Home*), is remarkable for Hindus for a number of reasons.

The first is the excellent example of leadership shown by Pope Francis. In this letter the pope takes the bold step of speaking decisively about the needs of the environment that we share, and of our common responsibility to care for it—and consequently to care for each other.

The second is the wholehearted support it shows for Mother Earth, known to Hindus as Mother Bhumi. This support is spiritual, moral, and practical. It asks for balance and harmony in vision and lifestyle, a worldview shared by all yogis. It offers a broadminded critique of modern worldviews and suggests solutions that are simple and universal.

The third is the offering of fraternity among all creatures and the clarification of biblical teaching on this issue. Hindus particularly appreciate the care for other living beings shown in this encyclical and the foundation it creates for deeper and more universal discourse on the sacred nature of life.

The fourth is how Pope Francis embraces other religions and cultures by acknowledging their essential environmental teachings. In this he displays a humility which opens a door to trust. His humility reaches out to others for help, emphasizing his assertion that we are connected and dependent, materially and spiritually.

With these messages the Holy Father has touched a common chord and has taken a lead in environmental discourse, raising its focus, its tone, and its importance. This dialogue is not dependent on the sciences but on an obligation to protect and contribute to the world we live in—and doing so primarily because it is the right thing to do. These are welcome messages for Hindus.

The Holy Father, right from the outset, identifies "the ethical and spiritual roots of environmental problems" (*Laudato Si'*, 9), an analysis very much in line with Hindu teachings. The idea of *dharma,* of nurturing responsibility and thoughtfulness— being to the fore of action in Hindu culture—inspires millions to consider our world and our place in it. Hindu responses to climate change and environmental discourse are thus not "reduced" (to echo Pope Francis's concern) to circumstantial evidence or statistical fact. While taking these things into account, *dharma* inspires a focus on what is the right thing to do for our families, our nations, and our planet. Moral decision and selfless motivation are the dharmic viewpoints which should determine our actions in the world.

The pope's call to simplicity, to consider "less as more," is fully in line with Hindu and dharmic thought. This is a most welcome encouragement for all spiritual people to lead the life they are inspired to lead, setting aside pressures to conform to a world in which they may feel morally uncomfortable, or compromised. The whole document consistently echoes this mood of detachment favored by Hindu *Sadhus* (holy people) and holy people of all persuasions. Concluding that this "implies avoiding the dynamic of dominion and the mere accumulation of pleasures" (222), Pope Francis positively captures the relationship of service to the Supreme shared by many spiritual practitioners.

His call for the recognition of the value of virtue in education is most welcome, and one of the most important recommendations made in the encyclical. It is a message that will have a broad reach and can certainly inspire concern and care for our planet and all who live on Her.

Pope Francis' analysis of how current thinking often reduces our problems to the material, proposing mostly technological solutions, portrays the heart of a man who has dedicated his life to the hearts of others, to their essential needs and concerns. The fraternity of his namesake, St. Francis, the vocabulary of father, mother, sister, and brother, personalizes the world in which we live. By drawing all creatures close, by giving them a name and a face, we make it difficult to be cruel and harmful—to reduce them to commodities. It allows us to practice *ahimsa,* to minimize our violence, cruelty, and harm—our negative impact on the world and on those with whom we share the world.

In questioning human domination of the planet, and of other living beings, Pope Francis opens up an area of discussion most relevant to Hindus—the primacy of life. Offered in the spirit of dialogue invited by the encyclical, one observes that while the Holy Father's discourse is based on virtues of compassion and toleration, it is equally based on the principle of human dignity. This principle—while increasingly important for humankind as the basis of our legal, social, and environmental policies—may not be the best principle to use for the equitable treatment of others living beings. It may be that the principle of dignity for all living beings serves us better as a global community. Hindu thought, and that of others, would propose that the sacred nature of all life, and equality based on this universal principle, could better protect us from policies that lead to discrimination, exploitation, cruelty, and speciesism, the latter being a grave blind spot in common understanding.

Drawing our attention to the interconnections we share and our dependence on the laws of nature, the Supreme, and each other, the Holy Father emphasizes the quality and depth of these relationships. This is a subject at the core of many Hindu traditions. From one perspective, Hindus will often make the analysis that as very small participants in a wonderfully vast and complex creation we must acknowledge our starting point as being one of servants—very small cogs in a huge machine.

In nature we are invited to find how we can contribute to the greater whole, to the greater good, leaving aside thoughts of mastery, and thus establish the basis of all our relationships in the mood of service. This approach determines our relationship with nature as one of service, not of domination, as argued by Pope Francis, and yet not even of stewardship, but one in which we recognize our humble position in the scheme of things and act accordingly.

From another perspective, many Hindu traditions treat our relationship with the world as part of our relationship with the Supreme Lord. In the stories of Krishna and Rama we see the intimate connection between the avatar, God in a spiritual form, and all nature: rivers, oceans, mountains, forests, humans, animals, birds, and aquatics. Everyone and everything is intimately connected with God, who has arranged the wonderful facility of this manifest creation. The relationship is one of kindness and love.

Through our Lord we are thus interconnected and will naturally affectionately treat his nature as his garden, his farm, and his store of jewels. We will also acknowledge how our use of his resources of sun, wind, water, gas, stone, and oil are a loan of the Lord's property, to be used wisely, for the greater good, and to be replenished. By this approach, where God is a person, and all about us is personalized, we will not cause harm to rivers, to mountains, to forests, all personified in Hindu thought, or to brother tree or sister tiger.

With this worldview we see nature as our Mother, and thus the relationship remains one of service. We serve and respect our Mother Bhumi and help her in her service to the Supreme Lord.

To conclude, the global dialogue enthused by the generosity of spirit shown in this encyclical has only begun. It will offer many opportunities, challenges, and insights in time to come. I hope, by God's grace, that the inspiration of this initiative grows in influence and esteem. I thank the Holy Father for taking leadership in this field and infusing the environmental discussion with a message of hope, of personal assessment, and of love.

Shaunaka Rishi Das is the director of the Oxford Centre for Hindu Studies, Oxford, United Kingdom.

A Buddhist Response to *Laudato Si'*

By Brother Phap Man

"Every one of us can do something to protect and care for our planet. We have to live in such a way that a future will be possible for our children and our grandchildren. Our own life has to be our message."

—Thich Nhat Hanh, *The World We Have*

"Let justice roll down like water, and righteousness like an ever-flowing stream."

—Amos 5:24

The publication of *Laudato Si'*, Pope Francis' wonderful encyclical, touched me deeply.

I'm a Buddhist monk, born in the United States as a Christian. I was baptized at age 28 after being inspired by the teachings of the Buddhist teacher Thich Nhat Hanh to reconnect with my Christian roots. As the years went by, however, I felt powerfully drawn to Buddhist teachings and to the incredible gift they represented to me. Five years later, Thich Nhat Hanh initiated me at my monastic ordination ceremony by touching my head with water, surrounded by our community invoking the name of Avalokiteshvara—the bodhisattva, or awakened being, of great compassion. I have lived my life since then as a Buddhist monk, spending many years at our community in France.

There's a stream that runs through the forest into which our monastery is nestled; it comes down from a ridge that stands just above the monastery. We often walk along its banks on our daily round of silent walking meditation. It's a beautiful, quiet space. The earth is soft under bare feet. The sound of the stream blends with the melody of birdsong. Maples, hemlocks, and oaks form the roof and pillars of this forest temple. Sometimes I scoop up the water and wash my face and head, allowing the water to cleanse me, washing away cares and burdens. As I renew and restore my initiation, I recall a verse from one of my community's foundational texts, *Beginning Anew:*

"At the foot of the mountain there is a stream. Take the water and wash yourself, and you will be cured."

This is the water of justice and righteousness—of right mindfulness, and of the spirit of holiness, and healthy living. This is the healing water that I want to offer to myself, to us, to all brothers and sisters all over the planet in the face of the growing violence we enact on ourselves and our environment every day. This is what Pope Francis was seeking to do when he wrote *Laudato Si'*.

Pope Francis recognizes, as we all do, that we face grave, interconnected challenges. Nearly half the world's population of seven billion people lives without sufficient food, water, housing, health, or education. Unchecked industrial manufacturing, transport, and agriculture are rapidly depleting our world's resources, causing widespread pollution, deforestation, and global climate change. We see climate change already generating destructive super-storms and deadly heat waves. In coming decades, climate change will displace hundreds of millions of people, putting nations underwater, destroying ecosystems, and making barren large portions of arable land. Climate change, coupled with destructive agricultural and industrial processes, is precipitating the sixth great mass extinction in the history of life on earth. A significant percentage of all species on earth are likely to go extinct.

We are in deep need of a path of healing. The good news is that a path of healing is available. *Laudato Si'* describes this path from a Catholic perspective. Allow me to share several Buddhist teachings which may also be useful.

A core teaching of Buddhism is that finding the path of love based on truth and understanding can transform suffering into well-being and lasting happiness. According to this teaching, there is a right way of living, an ethical way of living, a path that can bring greater peace and happiness to people around the world. Indeed, a path of love and justice is available to us, to our world community. Together, we must seek this path.

Another Buddhist teaching is that the steps toward healing our broken society are available to all of us. Through a regular practice of mindfulness, we can awaken to the miracles of life right now in the present moment. Our tradition teaches us that we need time to give thanks, to touch wonder, beauty, and awe. Instead of turning on the television, or consuming something to cover up an unpleasant feeling, we can take a walk, take time to sit quietly, to pray, to be loved, and to love. We can spend time in our local wilderness or our local park. We can take time to visit a neighbor, care for what is around us. We can take time to do our next task mindfully with care, attention and reverence. As our hearts begin to open we may also find that we need time to cry in order to embrace and release the deep suffering we have been carrying. Many possibilities may begin to open up for us. This is the path of awakening.

A third Buddhist teaching is also relevant here—the Buddha's realization of dependent co-arising, that all things in the universe are interconnected, that we live in a state of interbeing. Understanding this interconnectedness, understanding that all our actions have consequences, is critically important in helping us become motivated to reduce our environmental impact. Cultivating the insight of interbeing and compassion, we will be able to act out of love, not fear, to protect our planet.

Everyday life can easily lead us to forget that our lives are inextricably interwoven with the natural world through every breath we take, the water we drink, and the food we eat. Through our lack of insight, we are destroying the very life-support systems that we and all other living beings depend on for survival.

Once we begin to take steps on the path of healing for ourselves, and consider our actions, then we will have the strength and capacity to connect to others, to build communities, and work together to protect each other and life on earth. We can shift the focus of our businesses from profit to innovation—to solving extraordinary problems, while creating lasting prosperity and sustaining the environment. We can examine our own consumption and purchases—what does it cost to produce the things we buy? We can begin to share resources, to work less, and to simplify our lives. We can begin to transform our educational system so that cooperation, community, and emotional intelligence are valued, so that we can offer opportunities to the underprivileged, so that we can teach respect and empower young women and young men to be happy and loving parents. We can connect to and learn from others: what are we doing that enriches life and makes it more beautiful?

There's no way to know for certain what will happen to our civilization. But one thing is certain: there are only benefits to be realized through a commitment to a path of love and justice. The love and happiness we generate will never be lost. This is the path of opening our hearts and making time to connect to each other and life all around us. The teaching on love is clear: love God, and love your neighbor as yourself. Today, as an interconnected community of seven billion—everyone is our neighbor. And God is among us in the smallest of things—a singing bird, a leaf, a blade of grass, a stone on the path. This is it—the moment for us to join together— the most precious moment of our lives.

As our Buddhist text teaches, at the foot of the mountain is a stream. Let us take the pure water of compassion and mercy, wash ourselves, and be healed. As the Bible says, Let justice flow down like water, and righteousness like an ever-flowing stream. May we all join together to protect the earth—our common home.

Brother Phap Man is a Buddhist monk in Zen Master Thich Nhat Hanh's International Plum Village Community and currently resides at Blue Cliff Monastery in the Shawangunk foothills of upstate New York.

A Jewish Response to *Laudato Si'*

By Rabbi Lawrence Troster

With the publication of *Laudato Si'*—already the most widely-read papal encyclical in church history—Pope Francis spoke powerfully not only to the Catholic community but to "people of good will" and to "every person living on this planet." He spoke not just as the leader of over one billion Catholics, but as a spiritual guide for everyone, believer and non-believer alike, and as perhaps the only person in the world with the potential to unite humanity to save itself and our increasingly fragile planet. Climate change is a universal human crisis that affects all of us, and the pope's encyclical is already having a major influence on international discussions on how to solve the environmental crisis. I sincerely believe that this is one of the best statements of a religious environmental perspective that has ever been written.

One of the central elements of the encyclical is the concept of integral ecology. Integral ecology refers to the idea that how we humans treat each other (human ecology) is intimately related to how we treat the earth and our fellow creatures (natural ecology). The pontiff explains that "every violation of solidarity and civic friendship harms the environment" (*Laudato Si'*, 142). He makes direct connections between our "throw-away culture" that pollutes and degrades the environment and how our society discards those "excluded" from the global economy, exploits workers, harvests human organs, and traffics in people. But he does not only critique our economic and political inactivity on the environmental crisis; he also offers a vision on how to create solutions: "I urgently appeal, then, for a new dialogue about how we are shaping the future of our planet. We need a conversation which includes everyone, since the environmental challenge we are undergoing, and its human roots concern and affect us all" (14).

As he explains integral ecology, Francis draws from the best of the Judeo-Christian tradition. He utilizes biblical teachings that have been quoted by Jewish and Christian eco-theologians for decades: from the Creation stories of Genesis 1 and 2 to the laws of the Sabbath, Sabbatical Year, and Jubilee in Exodus and Leviticus; expressions of awe and wonder in the book of Psalms; concern for justice from the prophets; the glory of Creation from the Wisdom literature, and the parables and life of Jesus from the Gospels.

Integral ecology is poetically best expressed in the Hebrew Bible in Psalm 148 (which Pope Francis utilizes in the encyclical) which is a creation hymn, probably a piece of Temple liturgy and a poetic map of the universe. The

Psalm's structure portrays Creation as being divided between a heavenly choir and an earthly choir. The heavenly choir includes the sun, moon, planets, and stars, whose role it is to praise God and to act as witnesses to a revelation of God. The earthly choir consists of the forces of the natural world, the landscape, animal life (both wild and domesticated), and all kinds of humans. They are copying the heavenly choir, uniting with them in the same role and singing the same song. Psalm 148 pictures human society as part of a community of worshippers whose purpose is to praise God. This is not only a physical order but also a moral order that connects all of our actions to the rest of life on the earth.

We are also made of the same stuff as other created things—the same atoms, the same subatomic particles—and therefore are kin to all things found in Creation. This means that we must not view other species "merely as potential 'resources'" but we are obligated to accept that they have inherent value. Every created thing gives God glory through its existence. When we interfere with this part of God's plan, through environmental degradation and species extinction, we are silencing other voices of the Creation choir, which is an offence to God.

Although the pope expresses a strong belief in the radical equality of all Creation, he also maintains a critical concept in Judaism, Christianity, and Islam: people are made in the image of God (Genesis 1:26. Hebrew: tzelem Elohim) and therefore have a special place and role in the Order of Creation. Of all God's creatures, only human beings have the power to disrupt Creation. This power comes from special characteristics that no other creature possesses (Psalm 8). In its original sense *tzelem Elohim* means that humans were put on the earth to act as God's agents and to actualize God's presence in Creation. But it also has ethical implications, which means that human beings have certain intrinsic dignities: infinite value, equality, and uniqueness. It also means that human beings possess God-like capacities: power, consciousness, relationship, will, freedom, and life. Human beings are supposed to exercise their power, consciousness, and free will to be wise stewards of Creation. They should help to maintain the Order of Creation even while they are allowed to use it for their own benefit within certain limits established by God (Genesis 2:14). Since the time of the expulsion from Garden of Eden, Creation has tended to be out of balance because of the human impulse towards inequality resulting from the misuse of its powers for selfish ends. And in the Hebrew Bible, the earth is morally sensitive to human misdeeds (Genesis 4, Leviticus 18:27-30).

As a rabbi, a parent, and a grandparent, I find that one of the most important topics of the encyclical reflects the pope's deep concern for intergenerational justice and solidarity. In a section called "Justice Between the Generations," he asks, "What kind of world do we want to leave to those who come after us, to children who are now growing up?" (160). For me, this is not an academic question, but one that lies at the heart of why I have been involved in this work for thirty years. For Pope Francis, "Intergenerational solidarity is not optional, but rather a basic question of justice" (159). So justice both horizontally (how we are morally connected to every person on the earth as well as non-human life) and vertically (intergenerational justice) is the most critical issue that lies at the heart of the environmental crisis. Environmental justice is concerned with the equitable distribution of risks and benefits, and the democratic participation in decision-making: in ethical terms, these are called "distributive justice" and "participatory justice." Both are critical to our discussion of the moral implications of climate change.

In the Jewish tradition there are many sources, starting with many of the laws of the Torah, that are concerned with the fair distribution of wealth and power. The Hebrew word for justice or equity is *Tzedek* which has a core meaning of equity. In the perfect world there is perfect equity in the political, economic, and justice systems. In the law codes in the books of Exodus, Leviticus, and especially Deuteronomy, there are many laws directed towards trying to redress the inevitable imbalances that human society produces. We should all be hearing and acting on the call from Deuteronomy: "Justice, justice you are to pursue in order that you may live and possess the land that the Lord your God has given you" (Deuteronomy 16:20). We have no right to the fruits of the earth without *Tzedek*.

The pope rightly sees climate change and other aspects of environmental degradation that have a disproportionate impact on the poor as a moral and spiritual crisis. His thoughtful critique of the modern economy, consumerism, the current concept of progress, and the way in which technology can have a negative impact on the environment if not properly regulated finds resonance with many of the justice laws of the Torah and the moral calls of the Prophets which express God's particular concern for the powerless and the poor.

The pope properly expresses that the responsibility for solving this crisis lies in our hands, not in a divine intervention or the end of days. There is a *midrash* (Rabbinic commentary on the Bible) to Ecclesiastes 7:13 (Consider God's doing! Who can straighten what has been twisted?) that Jewish environmentalists have been utilizing for decades:

"When God created the first human beings, God led them around the Garden of Eden and said: 'Look at my works! See how beautiful they are—how excellent! For your sake I created them all. See to it that you do not spoil and destroy My world; for if you do, there will be no one else to repair it' " (*Midrash Ecclesiastes Rabbah, 7:13*).

In the Jewish liturgy there is a prayer called *Aleinu* in which we ask that the world be soon perfected under the sovereignty of God (*le-takein 'olam be-malkhut Shaddai*). *Tikkun 'olam,* the perfecting or the repairing of the world has become a major theme in modern Jewish social justice theology. It is the partnership of humanity with God in solving the world's problems, but it is primarily a recognition of human responsibility for the fate of Creation. In our ignorance and our greed we have damaged the world and silenced many of the voices of the choir of Creation. Now we must fix it. There is no one else to repair it but us. *Laudato Si'* represents a great moral call to *Tikkun 'Olam*.

Rabbi Lawrence Troster is the founder of Shomrei-Breishit: Rabbis and Cantors for the Earth, and GreenFaith Rabbinic Scholar in Residence.

A Muslim Response to *Laudato Si'*

By Imam Zaid Shakir

Prophet Muhammad (peace upon him) is reported to have said, "Wisdom is the lost property of the believer; wherever he finds it, he claims it." Perhaps this is the reason Pope Francis' encyclical on the environment and climate change, *Laudato Si'*, has been so well received by our community. It is as if his wise leadership on this issue is helping to return a part of our lost heritage to us. As a community, we have long embraced ideas such as sustainability, viewing the earth as our common home, and seeing ourselves vouchsafed to protect, nurture, and beautify it. These are themes mentioned by the pope in his historic encyclical, and these are themes that inform the Islamic Climate Declaration, issued in August 2015.

These themes certainly resonate with Muslims. God has prepared the earth to be our home from the time Adam was sent to dwell herein (2:36). The Qur'an describes that preparation in the following moving words, "And the earth We spread out, and cast therein firm mountains, and We caused to grow therein all manner of things in due balance. And we placed therein means of livelihood for you and for those for whom you provide not. Naught is there, but that its treasuries lie with Us, and We did not send it down, save in a known measure. And We sent forth the winds, fertilizing. And We sent down water from the sky, providing you with sufficient drink thereby, and you are not the keepers of its stores" (15:19-22). The blessings mentioned here and the favors that flow from them make our life on this earth both possible and pleasurable.

These blessings allow us benefit in clear ways and they are the foundation of our physical existence. To allow them to be diminished, or possibly destroyed, threatens our physical existence. There is, however, a nonphysical level from which we can view these graces. To begin understanding that level, let us consider some basic Qur'anic teachings. God reminds us, "We did not create Heaven and Earth and whatsoever is between in play. We did not create them, save in truth" (44:38-39). We understand this verse to mean that this world was created for a definite purpose. One of those purposes, which is mentioned in another verse, is to glorify God. We read, "The seven heavens, and the earth, and whatsoever is in them glorify Him. There is nothing, save that it hymns His praise, though you do not understand their praise. Truly He is Clement, Forgiving" (17:44). Similarly, "Hast thou not considered that unto God prostrates whosoever is in the heavens and whosoever is on the earth, the sun, the moon, the stars, the mountains, the trees, and the beasts, and many among humankind" (22:18).

Such proclamations from the Divine help shape a *Weltanschauung* that looks beyond physical systems and immediately perceptible biological functions. They create awareness of a creation that is spiritually alive and finds its highest expression in the worship and adoration of its Lord. It glorifies God and sings His praises, by night and day. Hence, when we pollute the air, defile the land, or poison the water, we tear asunder delicate ecosystems working in incredible harmony with each other. By so doing, we not only destroy our worldly home, we interrupt the great symphony of praise that its denizens are engaged in. We disrupt their worship.

The Qur'an also informs us that the creation embodies a delicate balance, which we are enjoined to maintain. We read, "The Merciful taught the Qur'an; created the human; taught him speech. The sun and the moon are upon a reckoned [course], and the stars and trees prostrate. Heaven He has raised and the balance He has set, that you transgress not in the balance. So weigh justly and fall not short in the balance. The earth He has laid down for all creatures. Therein are fruits and date palms bearing sheaths, husked grains and fragrant herbs. So which of the favors of your Lord do you deny?" (55:1-13). This set of verses calls our attention to the heavenly order and the amazing signs it displays of Divine wisdom. They then call us to turn our gaze to the lower, more accessible world immediately surrounding us and the great favors and blessings God has bestowed upon us therein. We are reminded, however, that the perpetuity of those graces lies in maintaining the balance that defines them.

Excess and waste disrupt that balance and therefore interrupt the aforementioned worship that qualifies the natural order. In that sense, they are demonic. That the Qur'an therefore declares, "Truly the wasteful are the brethren of satans, and Satan is ungrateful to his Lord" (17:27), should not come as a surprise to us. We are to use and enjoy the resources of the earth. God encourages us, "O Children of Adam! Put on your adornment at every place of worship, and eat and drink, but do not be prodigal. Truly He loves not the prodigal" (7:31). When, however, we squander and waste them through prodigious practices and lifestyles we are behaving in a demonic fashion, far removed from the godly spirit that should dominate our lives.

As Muslims, we believe that we have a responsibility to our earthy home, serving as God's vicegerent on earth. What exactly is the role of that vicegerent? Many interpretations are mentioned, in response to the term, *Khalifah*, introduced in a verse that mentions Adam being sent down to dwell on earth (2:30). One of those interpretations is one who acts on behalf of God, having been duly deputized. One of the great responsibilities of this vicegerent is to preserve the order God has established in the earth. We humans are told, "And work not corruption on the earth after it has been set aright, but call upon Him in fear and hope. Surely the Mercy of God is ever nigh unto the virtuous" (7:56). The environmental implications of this verse are clearly stated in the following exegetical passage:

> "Working corruption upon the earth" may also be understood as referring to human actions that pollute or destroy the natural environment. The human ability to "work corruption upon the earth is juxtaposed here with the earth's having been set aright, that is, by God. God's "setting aright" can thus mean His establishment, through the revelations and laws brought by His messengers, of a just and moral social order as well as his creating the harmony and balance that pervades the natural order. In light of mankind's contemporary ability to corrupt the earth physically through environmentally destructive behavior, this verse might therefore also be taken to mean that human beings should not physically corrupt the earth after God has "set it aright" with regard to its beauty, its inherent balance and harmony, and its beneficence for mankind—all of which are alluded to in many places in the Qur'an. (*Study Qur'an,* 428)

Therefore, we can understand that among the greatest duties of God's vicegerents is to preserve the beautiful, balanced, harmonious, and beneficent order God has established in the natural world. Doing so is not only necessary for the perpetuity of these great blessings; it is also the foundation of a just and moral social order. It is not accidental that the unprecedented ecological damage being done to this planet is accompanied by unprecedented levels of economic disparities. This situation not only fuels the unnatural and increasingly dangerous changes in the earth's climate, it also fuels the growing political instability and the resultant wars, which pose a growing threat to our collective security.

As Muslims, as people of faith, we must stand up and take the lead in addressing the causes of climate change and the underlying environmental degradation that fosters it. Doing so will require a degree of environmental consciousness that is unprecedented both in its nature and scope. Creating that consciousness is a moral imperative, and it has always been the job of religion to provide the framework that supports society-wide higher morality and ethics. There are no substitute or alternative institutions capable of assuming this task. Hence, as people of faith, we will either rise to the challenge before us to provide moral leadership on this issue, or we will sit back as seemingly helpless spectators as the earth and human civilization as we have known them cease to exist. The choice is ours.

Imam Zaid Shakir is a Muslim American scholar, public speaker, and author who is a co-founder, senior faculty member and Trustee of Zaytuna College in Berkeley, California. He teaches courses on Arabic, law, history, and Islamic spirituality.

GreenFaith
Interfaith Partners in Action for the Earth

GreenFaith is a multi-faith environmental organization. We work with diverse religious and spiritual groups in the United States and internationally, educating, equipping, and mobilizing them to put their beliefs into action for the earth.

GreenFaith offers:

• Religious education materials linking faith and creation care

• Environmental leadership training for faith leaders

• Campaigns by faith communities to reduce pollution

• Environmental certification for parishes and faith communities

• GreenFaith Circles – local hubs of religious-based environmental action

www.greenfaith.org•info@greenfaith.org

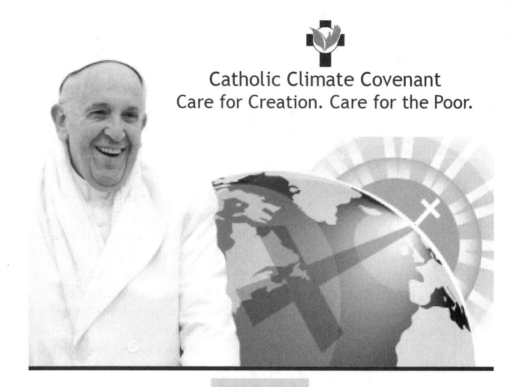

Catholic Climate Covenant
Care for Creation. Care for the Poor.

Catholic Climate Covenant helps Catholic people and institutions respond to the moral call for action on climate change. We open policy conversation, reduce carbon footprints, and share authentic Catholic teachings on climate change. Not only do Catholics care about climate change, we have the power to overcome it. At Catholic Climate Covenant, we build relationships between people with common values and a shared commitment to protecting the people and places we love.

To learn more and to help care for creation and care for the poor:

Visit: www.catholicclimatecovenant.org
Write to: info@catholicclimatecovenant.org

RESOURCES FROM
RENEW
INTERNATIONAL

RENEW
Small-Group
Leader Series

Essentials for Small-Group Leaders

This book offers a comprehensive collection of pastoral insights and practical suggestions to help small community leaders guide their groups in a way that nourishes spiritual growth. Culled from RENEW International's three decades of experience in pioneering and promoting small Christian communities, this book overflows with simple but effective ideas and strategies that will enhance the way these groups reflect on and respond to the Gospel.

Leading Prayer in Small Groups

Have you ever been asked to lead prayer for your church group, council, or committee? RENEW International has developed a helpful new resource called *Leading Prayer in Small Groups* to encourage you in leading fruitful group prayer experiences with confidence. *Leading Prayer in Small Groups* emphasizes the importance of group prayer for church groups of every kind and provides insight into why we pray. It also explains the role, qualities, and duties of a leader of prayer. Readers are guided through the stages of preparing group prayer and the process of effectively leading prayer for a group.

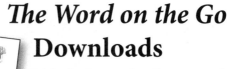

Theology on Tap

RENEW Theology on Tap offers an innovative solution to one of today's most pressing pastoral concerns: how to reach out to young Catholic adults. Young adults can sometimes be overlooked to the extent that even their absence goes unnoticed. **RENEW Theology on Tap** reaches young adults where they are, while inviting them to discover how faith can give sense to their everyday lives. It is a way for dioceses and parishes to discover (or rediscover) these young adults in comfortable, relaxed settings.

The Word on the Go Downloads

Faith-sharing session for young adults are focused on the Sunday gospel readings. The sessions are published individually for weekly faith-sharing sessions are are available only online.

For purchase and immediate download visit: **www.renewintl.org/store**

Campus RENEW

Campus RENEW is a two and a half year (or 5 semester) process which facilitates renewal and transformation on college campuses. Small Christian communities, groups of eight to twelve students who come together weekly to share faith, are the building blocks of this process. These communities create opportunities for students to experience community, spirituality, and be challenged outward to service. The Campus RENEW process creates student leaders with a mature faith and social consciousness to guide the Catholic Church both today and in the future. The result is a process which creates and nurtures small Christian communities on college campuses through leadership formation, quality faith sharing resources, and onsite and offsite pastoring.

La justicia brota de la fe

Formación en la Doctrina Social Católica de la Iglesia

La justicia brota de la fe es un proceso de formación para hispanos sobre el compromiso social y la íntima conexión entre la fe y el amor hacia el prójimo. Esta obra, en comunión con la Nueva Evangelización, promueve el desarrollo espiritual de todos los que anhelan profundizar la práctica de su fe en un ambiente tan desafiante como el de hoy.

Los dos libros del participante representan las creencias claves de la Doctrina Social de la Iglesia en el contexto de la Palabra de Dios y la diversidad de las experiencias vividas del pueblo hispano en los Estados Unidos. Dos libros de doce sesiones cada uno, conectan la fe y la vida con reflexiones, preguntas para compartir, oraciones, y recomendaciones de las acciones a seguir.

RENEW
Scripture
Series

Luke: My Spirit Rejoices!

Luke: My Spirit Rejoices! is the first book in the RENEW Scripture Series. Written by scripture scholar Martin Lang, this faith-sharing book engages readers with the entire Gospel and includes reflections on the content of the Gospel, the human behavior illuminated in Luke's work, and the Old Testament background for each passage. Sharing questions and opportunities to apply the gospel message to daily life make this a perfect resource for small Christian communities. Can be used individually or in a group.

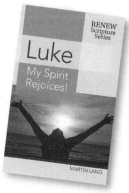

Matthew: Come Follow Me

The Gospel of Matthew is the first book in the New Testament, a distinction that reflects high value the Church has placed on this Gospel for nearly two thousand years. *Matthew: Come Follow Me* explores this unique account of the ministry, passion, and glorification of Jesus. Written by scripture scholar Martin Lang, each chapter includes reflections on the Gospel plus sharing questions and examples of how the teaching of Jesus may apply to our everyday lives. This is a perfect resource for small groups, for personal reflection, or for homily preparation.

For more information go to **www.renewintl.org/scripture**

Spirituality
for Everyday Life
with RONALD ROLHEISER

Experience how the gentle spiritual guidance and practical wisdom of best-selling Catholic author Fr. Ronald Rolheiser, OMI can enliven everyday life.

Longing for the Holy is a series of reflections based on Ronald Rolheiser's *The Shattered Lantern* and *The Holy Longing.* Fr. Rolheiser describes three stages of discipleship: 1) Getting your life together; 2) Giving your life away; and 3) Giving your death away. *Longing for the Holy* covers different dimensions of contemporary spiritual life for those who want to enrich their sense of the presence of God and develop a deeper spirituality in the first stage of discipleship.

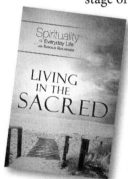

Living in the Sacred takes participants on a deeper spiritual journey exploring the second stage of discipleship: "Giving your life away," as described in Fr. Rolheiser's *Sacred Fire*. Having moved through the "getting your life together" stage participants have made life commitments either in marriage or other relationships, child raising, to sick or elderly parents or other relatives, careers, communities. *Living in the Sacred* is about how we stay true to these commitments as disciples of Christ.

For more information visit **www.renewintl.org/spirituality**

Be My Witness:
Formation for the New Evangelization

The New Evangelization represents a special opportunity for leaders in the Church—helping baptized Catholics embrace their role in passing on the flame of faith and setting hearts on fire to bring Christ's warmth and light to all.

Get the conversation started in your parish about the single most important topic facing our Church today—evangelization. *Be My Witness* is a Christ-centered, Spirit-led process that draws its inspiration from *The Joy of the Gospel*, Pope Francis' landmark document on evangelization.

All the resources for *Be My Witness* are also fully available in Spanish as *Sean mis testigos: Formación para la Nueva Evangelización*.

Learn more and contact us to bring *Be My Witness* to your parish: **www.bemywitness.org**

Be My Witness gives parishes the power to build an ever-widening circle of conversion and commitment by engaging both parish staff and leaders, as well as parishioners, in two phases.

In the first phase, parish leadership is guided through the transformation process with training and consultation including:

- Leader guides
- Parish assessment tools
- Video-based learning modules
- Online training and web resources
- RENEW staff support.

In the second phase, small-group members develop the attitudes and behaviors of missionary disciples with:

- 12-session participant book
- Video DVD with real-life witness stories.

All the resources for *Be My Witness* are also fully available in Spanish as *Sean mis testigos: Formación para la Nueva Evangelización.*

Watch our free webinar: **bemywitness.org/explore**

ARISE Together in Christ

is a three-year, parish-centered process of spiritual renewal and evangelization that enables people to deepen their faith, develop a closer relationship with Christ, grow in community, and reach out in service to others. It emphasizes people living in good relationship with one another, as they make concrete applications of the Gospel to their life situations.

ARISE Together in Christ is a total renewal experience for the parish, spiritually transforming people through small Christian communities, special parish activities, reflections for families with teens and children, and Christian social action. There are five six-week seasons:

Season One: **Encountering Christ Today**

Season Two: **Change Our Hearts**

Season Three: **In the Footsteps of Christ**

Season Four: **New Heart, New Spirit**

Season Five: **We Are the Good News!**

For each Season, RENEW International offers a faith-sharing book and a music CD with the songs suggested in the faith-sharing book.

The faith-sharing books are designed principally for use by adults; however, they are complemented by materials for children and for youth. Both are designed around the same themes and the same Scripture passages as in the adult books.

ARISE for youth

Faith-sharing materials for each session of all five Seasons, written especially for youth. Also includes a separate ARISE for youth Leader Guide.

ARISE Family Sharing Pages

A friendly easy way to explore the same faith themes at home and in class. Four-page, full color worksheet for each session of each Season. Available for Grades 1-3, and Grades 4-6.

WHY CATHOLIC?
Journey through the Catechism

is a parish-based process of evangelization and adult faith formation from RENEW International. This process, designed for sharing in small Christian communities, is structured around exploring the important truths of our faith as they are presented in the *Catechism of the Catholic Church* and in the *United States Catholic Catechism for Adults*.

WHY CATHOLIC? helps nourish faith and enhance our sense of Catholic identity. The process and materials encourage us to understand and live the reasons why we are Catholic, and so lead us to a faith that is experienced more authentically, connecting us more deeply and meaningfully to God, and to others.

There are four books in the *WHY CATHOLIC?* series, each offering twelve sessions:

> *PRAY: Christian Prayer*
>
> *BELIEVE: Profession of Faith*
>
> *CELEBRATE: Sacraments*
>
> *LIVE: Christian Morality*

WHY CATHOLIC? is far more than printed resources for faith-sharing in small communities. It is a complete integrated process providing materials and support both in print and on the web, together with opportunities for faith enrichment events and retreats for the whole parish, as well as a series of training workshops for small community leaders.

For each of the four *WHY CATHOLIC?* books, there is a Song CD. Each CD is a 12-song compilation of the songs suggested for the moments of prayer during the faith-sharing sessions. The CDs are available singly, or as a set.

Families can extend the fruits of the sharing on the same themes presented in the books by using *RENEWing Family Faith*: attractive four-color companion bulletins with activities and reflections for sharing among different age groups.

For more information or to order

these and other fine resources from RENEW International, please visit our secure online bookstore at **www.renewintl.org/store** or use our toll free order line: **1-888-433-3221.**

Tom + Rita, Marilyn, Kathy, Sandy, Peggy, Carol? me
blond-short cut   short   gray pony   mid-length   red hair
Katherine   gray   tail   blondish   choir
headband

For June - 27th, 1 pm

"First 31 ¶ of Laudato Si, + see p. 8

The Art of Saving the Planet" by Thich Nat Kan

Heartland" ~ TV show w/o sex, etc

Hope" by Jane Goodall